EMPOWERMENT
AND CHANGE

EMPOWERMENT AND CHANGE

B THOMAS MILLER

Library of Congress Control Number:		2019904619
ISBN:	Hardcover	978-1-7960-2873-7
	Softcover	978-1-7960-2872-0
	eBook	978-1-7960-2871-3

Rev. date: 04/17/2019

To order additional copies of this book, contact:
Xlibris
1-888-795-4274
www.Xlibris.com
Orders@Xlibris.com
795603

CONTENTS

Introduction

The purpose of this work is to create a positive change in life. People at times will feel a sense of hopelessness and anxiety because the person wants to make a change but for some reason likes the tools in life to make the change. This book offers a guide to help those who may some support in this endeavor. The text of love created because this psychologist observes people who seem to be on a proverbial gerbil wheel of life and seem not to be going and where but wasting energy and wasting time here on earth.

This book based on a three-step approach which is subjective to the reader interpretations and the path which works best for her/him. This psychologist believes the best method in this short life makes the best of each day. People look at the past and have an eye on the future, but this psychologist affirmation is people need to live in the present. The goal in life as well as to make the best of each day and live the day as it is your last.

Empowering and Change is the title of the book. Enabling can change people's look on life if the person uses the right mental framework to make the proper changes. People who have low-self-esteem or people have negative thoughts can benefit significantly from this book. Coaches can benefit from this as well because this psychologist believes coaching is generic. People of all walks of life profess to be coaches of change, but this psychologist observes for change to occur the person has to commit and want the difference in life.

This book will offer insights to all. To all my friends and family I dedicate this book. Thank you for the love which inspired me to be a better person and physiologist.

Chapter One

Empowering And Change

The purpose of drafting this book is how to improve one's life. This psychologist likes the word empowerment which allows a person to take charge of their life. A person who engages in their life lives happier and fulling life which helps the person to be in charge of promoting their experience. The results in enabling are the person becomes confident and stronger. When one becomes stronger and can take charge of the day, this leads to controlling their lives. Contemporary times when people think of empowering other people to think of the education system. Empowering students has been part of the education system for some time. Allowing children to be responsible for learning and for seeing the progress in their knowledge enables the child to be a better student. Educating children and believing in their accomplishments enhances children to follow their dreams. The same is right for individuals, letting individuals be responsible for the correct choices in life and teaching how to live a better life is a dream of this psychologist.

The reason for this project is watching my triplet girls becoming responsible ladies and how as a psychologist to achieve their best and be their best in life. This psychologist professes this with people who interact daily and as well as friends and family. His goal in life to help those make a change in their lives. This author sees as he has learned himself, the first step in any decision is taking personal responsibility.

Part of life focuses on studying and working hard to achieve wealth and success. This author enforces the value of following one's dreams and pontificate this to his girls, family, and friends. Achieve anything in life; it takes a 100% effort every day. Part of the process in "seizing the day focuses on empowering one's day. Empower may seem like a new word, but the word exists since the 17th century.

Empowering refers to helping individuals achieve success in life by realizing their abilities and potential to make positive changes in their lives. People often feel trapped or a feeling of hopelessness sets into their personality and feel they have nowhere to turn or to get help. Empowerment and transforming one's negative thoughts to positive can transform lives by taking personal responsibility. Further, this creates a change in the presence in the person and which reflects those around the person. How did empowerment manifest its self and how does it apply to this modernity?

Empowerment originates from social psychology and associates with social scientist Julian Rapport (1981) who introduced the concept of empowerment into social psychology and social work. His work, In Praise of A Social Policy of Empowerment Over Prevention, depicted how paradoxical community life can be to an individual. Additionally, social problems require nonexperts to turn to experts to discover the many different, even Paradox contradictory solutions that individuals will use to gain control, thus find meaning and empowering their lives to a better experience. The social disconnect occurs with people who tend to low-income and low education.

The author is not trying to commend the low-income or low-educated, the fact this is further from the truth the goal here is to improve peoples lives through education and empowerment to make a difference in their lives and family. Cultural and economic gaps amongst people are widening. Cultural differences are not just a national issue or a geographical issue but a global issue. Though certain scholarly writings suggest, this is a Marxist approach this is further from the truth. Social strife is more of a practical method of not taking advantage of lower classes and forming a classless society where everyone has an opportunity to succeed and be empowered to achieve wealth and happiness.

Low-income and low education tends to go hand to hand. One other problem among low-income and small social order are people have at least some form of addiction such as cigarettes, illegal drugs, or alcohol to help the people cope with their everyday life. Though the author sees all the high styles as enablers in people lives the substances deter the individual from achieving a higher growth for themselves. This psychologist sees this in daily life as people who smoke would get cigarettes before putting gas in the tank. Society has a loss of its compass and people in the low-income are feeding programs such as the lottery and tobacco tax. This psychologist depicts in the big picture of society, disregard to the low-income occurs because money is spent mainly in the suburbs where people pay the fees. Since the tax revenue goes to the state or federal level most of the time, the people who need the assistance go neglected or the social programs are limited to budget cuts in the federal and state level. This author calls the tax "poor man's tax." The objective to change an individual by letting go of the taxes in poor neighborhoods or remove the problem such as the lottery or the cigarette tax.

The lottery, for example, is used for example because a person "thinks" riches will come their way. When in actuality, the state makes most of the revenue, and the impulsive, sick person stays poor. This psychologist believes the removal of the lottery system can enable poor neighborhoods to ina better existence. The goal is to teach people to save and to be empowered. No impulsive behavior helps growth. People need to learn patience and self-worth.

The roots of empowerment also intersect the empowerment theory. Other authors such as Karl Marx discuss the power empowerment such as in his Marxist Theory. The is psychologist sees Utilitarian Theory as more inlined in empowerment. As stated by, Five Ways To Shape Ethical Decisions: the Utilitarian Approach, depicts empowerment by assesses an action in terms of its consequences or outcomes; i.e., the net benefits and costs to all stakeholders. The individual is the main focus in a Utilitarian Theory. This psychologist argues the value in collectivism theory over individualistic theory because the society as a whole has let down the working poor. Observing the class structure in today's world. The middle-class is shrinking, and the low-class is growing. Soon the structure will be of those who have the opportunities and those who do not have the chance to grow and prosper. Collectivism focuses on the importance of the whole culture, but the value is in the individual awareness is critical. Low-income people can not enable themselves out of the low-class structure so the consequences the people develop a sense of hopelessness and despair.

Remember the focus of this body of work is to change the person in being more empowered. And create change in their life. This work focuses on the individual rather than the society or the class structure. There is a distinction between the values that underline an empowerment approach to social change and how the move is part of the empowerment theory. Personal values shift leads to the beginning of empowerment and suggest aims and strategies forever lasing significant variation. The empowerment theory provides principles and framework for organizing one's knowledge. The point of this first half of this work is to put into motion the context they, into place while empowering will put the framework into action.

This psychologist argues there are many divisions within psychology. Though this author is an I/O psychologist, the framework of this project leans heavily in social psychology. The emphasis in empowerment lies within the individual and for the individual to change her/his life through professional approach, training, and development, which align with this author's specialty in I/O psychology. The goal is personal growth is in the perspective of the individual, and the empowerment and change occur in a specific area in private life. This author would argue a micro-change.

In psychology, there is a difference between the micro and the macro level phenomena. The difference in this phenomenon can create an understanding of communities' woes and help create a plan of action for people who want to improve their lives. For example, micro examines the small-scale information such as the individual or small groups; on the other hand, macro refers to larger scale information such as a community or a metropolitan area. For this purpose, this author plans to address the micro issues within the individual. The objective is to change the individual's core belief, a and empowerment and change occur. This author believes once a "group" of people change their core beliefs, empowerment can improve a community. The outcome is one person can make a difference in a town or society; case in point t is Rosa Parks refusal to give up her seat on a bus.

Empowerment is a technique which used correctly analyzes the individual to make the correct changes in life. The author sees the value in empowerment and how the method can alter one's perception in their environment. The interaction in the environment affects the individual. Hence the micro, and how she/he can make the correct adjustments to increase their positive energy within the context: this author likes to call this method the social change empowerment. Key is to find the linchpin, the source of the negativity in mind, within an individual. Once the negativity is detected, the person can make the exact change to be more empowered and increase their self-esteem. This author developed a three-step process to help roadmap the shift in behavior and hence increase empowerment.

Chapter Two

Each of the following three-step processes is easy to understand and comprehend, but as stated above, empowerment is very subjective and personal. What empowers one person, such as weight loss, may not be as important as someone who needs to gain weight. But in each case, a change can create positive energy and a positive mindset. An individual's life can be empowered by following the three-step approach. Results can build a better experience for themselves and increase their self-esteem and self-awareness. Below is a list of eight empowerment quotes which opens the mind for change and creates growth for the individual. The citations also increase a positive mindset and remove and works on eliminating negativity in mind.

Eight things can create positive empowerment:

1. Be open to possibilities
2. Focus on the person one wants to be
3. Run one's race
4. Trust oneself
5. Network with others
6. One loves their mission they do in life
7. Be grateful in everything and everybody
8. Embrace imperfect moments

The above eight, when involved in one's life, can have an impact on one's life but the positive energy can encourage action and empower their lives as well. The goal is to understand how to change behavior which can have an impact and improve one's experience.

Number one addresses always keep open the possibilities. Eventually, people discourage or create a blockage in their mind, so the opportunity passes them by. Often when keeping open the chance the situation by the divine appears to the individual.

Number two centers the focus on the individual and focus who one is becoming. Individuality is where a person looks at their strengths and weaknesses and decides on the right action to change. When a person knows themselves well right action can happen fast.

Number three focuses on run one's race. The goal here is to look at anyone's goals and objective and create a strategy which gets them to move their life forward. The person does not look at others but only their lives.

Number four, addresses deal with trusting one's self and trusting your intuition. The goal here is to learn what the mind is telling someone. The goal is to examine the conscious and the subconscious where information tells one about an event. Have the correct people in one's influence circle. Remove negative people, and positive people added.

Number five is networking which enhances empowerment by reaching out and creating a mentor/teaching framework. A psychologist sees the value in helping others which increases one's empathy for others and increase self-awareness. Form a support group of "like-minded" empowering people.

Number six is loved what one does in life. A psychologist has found people who enjoy what they do in life and are happy and more enthusiastic in life. The key here, like anyone in life, is to see what makes a person happy and be willing to share this with others in one's life.

Number seven is always grateful in one's life and be willing to say I am sorry, please forgive me, and thank the person. The goal in life is to live and be grateful for every day. Live the most of each day and always bring the best of the person each day.

Number eight, embrace imperfect moments focuses on we are all imperfect and as a human being will make mistakes now and then. The goal is to take responsibility and to correct the situation as soon as possible.

The goal here is to analyze the positive empowerments and figure which can have the most significant impact in the shortest time. Even if the individual picks just one of the eight, the one can create deep thought and reflection and create a change and rise in empowerment. This psychologist would recommend two or three, and they chose the ones who have the most significant impact. What one is doing is creating a foundation for positive experiences. Life is about the positive experiences and aking a difference in their life and the life of others. What a person needs to do is analyze their social environment or what this psychologist likes to call his social empowerment change.

Social empowerment analyses the core of one's being and results in the transformation by critical thinking assessment and reflective assessment. Critical thinking is applying one's self-knowledge, what works for them and against them in life, by using the knowledge and social sciences, such as social psychology, to create an argument or theory. The case is the individual wants to change her/his life. Reflective assessment is what change can an individual make to create a happier life. In essence, the individual is reflecting on what two or three changes she/he can make to change their life around, what the reflective mode set into motion the individual's life becomes empowered and she/ he can reverse the negative mindset to a positive mindset.

This scholar plans to argue if one is committed to adding empowerment to their lives, the transformation will change the individual. Further, this therapist understands people need to step out of their comfort zone and keep an open mind. This scholar knows this can be scary and difficult. For example, the "working poor' may see their social environment and life, at times as hopeless and scary. Still, other "low income" does not know how to get "unstuck" or do not know where to turn for help. Social workers can help with the social aspect of a change in one's life, but a psychologist is committed to making a mental change in personal life, so thinking becomes a positive experience. One the person is committed to the change, positive thinking for individual emerges.

Within low-income communities, certain behaviors exist with the majority of people because of their daily existence and struggles throughout the day. What happens is impulsive behavior, and instant gratification emerges because the person needs some euphoria, such as drugs or alcohol, to exist. For example, in the case of Native Americans, as well as the inner city communities, people have an instant gratification problem, but some may have additions which the individual can not control. In these communities, patience and absence need teaching as a control mechanism against instant gratification. Individuals can make the correct changes in life for themselves and those who surround their inner-circle by empowering themselves and developing a better lifestyle. A better lifestyle is not smoking, drinking, and eating a well-balanced meal throughout the week.

The goal in this empowering project is for the person to comprehend how the person can change their lives and how the impact in change and empowerment can and will impact their immediate family and the community which she/he resides. The objective is simple in the approach by empowering one person; the goal is the one person enable someone else, and that person enables someone else. The result is a chain of self-empowered and self -assured individuals within a given community. The goal is to create a close-knit group of people who can help and inspire each other. A strong support base is critical in low-income areas or areas where crime and blight rule the neighborhoods. Empowerment is for all people and all walks of life. Empowerment has in the past connected with the education of children.

Empowerment focuses on education and social work. Both professional practica use a systematic approach based on a resource-oriented intervention. For example, social work involvement may focus on early childhood intervention. Charitable work programs are active in low-income communities. Empowerment is a concept towards a strength-oriented perception, by the individuals, and the underlying foundation is a management control concept. The person is to teach the individual skills which will enable the person to handle the day to day stresses in life and to work out an action plan to achieve self-worth and self-esteem within their specific communities. Self-esteem and self-worth is a micro approach and not a macro approach. The process in micro focuses on the individual. This author believes if a person creates the empowerment the effect will generate a change in the community as a whole and more people will be inspired to make change within their community. There are several different types of empowerment the six most common types are

Below are six forms of empowerment which can have an impact on self-growth and the rise in self-esteem and personal motivations:

Empowerment focuses on the person wants and needs. The discussion below will discuss the differences between the two. Additionally focuses on changing peoples core beliefs.

Economic Empowerment focuses on creating personal wealth.

Political Empowerment focuses on how a person organizes and how that process helps the individual make correct decisions.

Cultural Empowerment understands other cultures, and the impact can enhance the understanding of different cultures.

Societal Empowerment focuses on understanding society and how social communities have an impact on personal life.

National Empowerment focuses on understanding the national culture and a form and rising in 'nationalism."

For this project in writing, the author plans to address the first empowerment which focuses on individuals wants and needs. The discussion will focus on the differences in desire and requirements and a bottom-up approach for individuals. The goal in any empowerment program is to change their behavior to a positive mindset instead of a negative mindset. The positive change behavior will create empowerment for the individual which will result in higher self-esteem and personal motivation. As one can see, there are different approaches in empowerment, and just like psychology, each therapist will offer their unique perspective, each empowerment address a particular area of concern. Empowerment, in the belief of this psychologist, is a bottom-up process. Bottom-up refers to the way an individual builds up the smallest pieces of sensory information.

Further, the person learns the necessary knowledge and moves up the information network. This psychologist believes this is the best approach to teach empowerment and change people with low-self esteem and low motivation. Right people for this study are Native Americans which this researcher is currently working to help improve their lives.

Top-down processing, on the other hand, is the perception that is driven by thought processes. The brain interprets the information and applies what the mind knows and what the spirit is willing to accept as truth. This psychologist believes this form of the building is complex and a person has to have high self-esteem and be aware of their strengths and weaknesses. Since this project is on empowering, the top-down would be impractical for people with low-self esteem people. This approach is more suited for small organizations, and the people are well connected emotionally and spiritually to each other and involved in their work environment.

Like a building a house, a person has to build the brain and build it correctly; the smallest part of the mind is sensory nodes which release negative and positive energy. Negative nodes, such as negative thoughts, can build up in the brain and enhance the negative thoughts. Build up some much negative energy can lead to issues in depression and anxiety. At times the sensory nerves can be the culprit for the negative thoughts and the feeling of hopelessness. This three-step process this therapist develop focuses on changing the negative energy to positive. The stronger the positive sensory nerve information and the higher the cognitive level. This higher level leads to one's perceptions of feelings and emotions called empathy. Blockage can occur at low negative energy as well.

This author believes why some students failed at a given subject, such as math because there are the sensory blocks the information that tells she/him that they can not do the math! This psychologist offers a three-step process will increase cognitive levels and change positive behavior which the person would like to see.

The results from this author 's three-step approach are for the individual to increase their empowerment and positive which will occur. The change in empowerment will create a positive difference in an individual's life. Empowerment is subjective and personal. As stated above, this therapist goal is to create a "road map" to helps individual to improve their lives. This psychologist has worked with people and sees the "look" in the eye when the person in charge of their life. Real change can be time-consuming and does require a lot of time and thoughtful meditation.

This psychologist depicts how people tend to be creatures of habit, even this psychologist, at times, like to take the easy road. The result in change focuses on going from point A to point B. The process of change can be a short duration, or the change may take a year. This psychologist refers a time when he broke up with a woman he cared about as "his lost years." I believe John Lennon had this time after leaving the Beatles he was called the "Lost Weekend." The point or the clique of lost weekends and or lost years are when negative thoughts consume one's life and control their life over specific ideas. The goal here is to remove the lost weekends and years and be present and positive in life.

Chapter Three

People often as this therapist, "How can a person change a negative thought into a positive thought? How can a transformation occur for a negative individual? Can a positive change influence those around the individual to make changes in their life as well? The answer to these questions is yes. The move to positive is affected by focusing on the positives in life and dealing with the present rather than thinking of the negative and dwelling in the past. People as the clique says have a lot of baggage. For some, the weight can be daunting, so the key is to lose the luggage and think positive. Anybody who has a positive mindset can make any changes in life. Positive thoughts create windows of opportunities in life.

The positive change is based on a framework to improve her/his life. The focus in any situation is what can this teach me about this situation. Instead of dwelling in the past or cynical mode look at it in a positive mode. Ask the question, how can this person change this experience into a positive experience. For example, in the rise of social media, it can be difficult at times to be positive when working around people who are always negative and the people. One reason for a detrimental deposition is people are afraid of the unknown, and this enhances their anxiety into negativism. The rationale for change occurs when people have reached in a pass in life or their life is "rock bottom," and the person doesn't know how why the anxiety or stress in their life. One way to combat the problem is mediation or reflection in life.

The focus of this book is to understand why and when people feel "stuck" in their life. Why does anxiety or depression intensify the situation when people feel a sense of hopelessness? People approach this author and often ask what a person can do to change their outlook, i.e., such as changing their attitude in life. People often see my positive approach and have a way of lighting up a room. The answer to the question above is people need to get out of their comfort zone, and people need to think and feel positive every day. The problem with some individuals is they exhibit patterns of anxiety because they are afraid to step out of their comfort zone. Feeling comfortability is easier because stepping out of their 'comfort zone" can be daunting and scary. The fact this psychologist is writing a book which illustrates people getting out of his comfort zone by doing something she/he is not comfortable doing. For example, getting up at 5 am to go exercise takes a lot of energy and guts especially if you are a night person. The person has decided to set out of their comfort zone.

Writing an extraordinary book like this takes time and discipline. My weekly goal is 35 pages per week with a final book count of at least 120 pages. To complete a book requires dedication: control, and a strategy to accomplish this project. In any project, the goal is learning from the competition and finding what works in a project and what did not work in the project. Additionally, counting on a reliable support system will enhance one's positive energy and bring out the best in the person. Finally, having goals and objectives and where one sees the progress of the task at hand. The goal is developing a plan of action.

A solid plan removes the negativity, and the focus becomes positive because one is completing the given task. Negativity and distractions are an everyday occurrence in life. This therapist experiences negativity as well, but the objective he has learned is to control the negative energy and karma patterns in his mind. Tasks can be complicated and bothersome and are not easy, and to some, it can seem like the task 'sucks" or as this psychologist likes to state, "it's like one big gerbil wheel." You keep spinning and spinning, and one seems to go nowhere. This belief is among all people, all races, and over the globe is a feeling of hopelessness and daily anxiety and or depression. Part of the problem in the modern world is the rise of social media and the need for self-gratification. An example of this is watching the cable news if a national emergency occurs; it is 24-hour coverage, and the networks try to do each other in coverage out. During the election night when one system will call a race while the other does not.

This psychologist observation illustrates, people all over the globe, tend to live in this instant gratification society. This psychologist believes with the rise of social media and the increase in world wide web people demand things in an instant. For example, one can order products online, such as Amazon Prime, and the products will arrive at their location within hours. One can see the ads on the social and cable networks which portray buy this "right now," and this will change one's life. For example, people can analyze these ads such as beer commercials and car commercials. Drink this certain beer and one will be the envy of the neighbors and attractive the "perfect" mate. The person buys these things and except changes will occur but in actually things stay the same. The ads play on people's egos because the ego likes happiness and success. The product does not give a "feeling" of success, but the person is trying to do changes in their life and sees little results. The commercial and ads on television and social media do not tell the whole story, Wealth and happiness come from within, and one cannot obtain without the correct mindset.

The downside of these ads does not discuss the consequences of one's purchase has on their own physical and mental ability. The ads forget to mention the "hangover" the next day or the car payment which could devour your monthly income. The sad fact is those who buy the item, inhale, or digest the products found the success does not come easy. The goal is impulsive buying but then as the clique says, "buyer's remorse." Companies understand and play with people in this instant success mode. The goal for example, for male enhancement for more prolonged, lasting sexual intercourse when in fact the problem may be a mental block or an issue of anxiety or being over-stressed.

Another example is looking at the weight loss products on the market. The goal is to make the person be "happy" with their body and to a certain extent higher self-esteem. Once an individual uses the product or joins a gym, for example, the road to success is not an instant makeover. This process makes not take days but years. For example, gym memberships increase after the first of the year, New Year Resolutions, but by April many of the people stop going to the gym regularly. People get this sense of "hopelessness "and say well this is what my life is meant to be and give up or settle for less than what one can achieve. Working out at the gum takes time, and the results take time as well, so people develop a "false hope" and for those who want a change, are dedicated and persistent in their weekly and monthly goals. Persistence in a person is willing to stick the process out into completion no matter what is happening in their lives. Therefore, weekly and monthly goals and objectives are essential to complete the given goals, and the tasks must be a challenge. People tend to give up within a few short days without seeing much success. Working hard and being persistent is part of the growth process.

Here again, people want instant success. People need patience and willing to work on the days when they do not feel the benefits of working out can offer any benefit to the individual. Mel Robbins believes there is a lot of days one does not feel like, so the goal is to not to complain and complete the task. Admiral McGarven thinks stop complaining, and he calls this complaining a "sugar cookie, so stops complain and seize the day! What happens people give up, and hopelessness sets in and the fear of being stuck and feelings of negative emotions overwhelm the person. Negative emotions and thoughts do not have to capture the person day or ruin their day. People are in charge of their day and not the negative feeling which does not, have to be the case. It is about seeing one's mind on the right directional course. For example, when this author gets upset with himself, he speaks aloud that he a dumbass or such so naïve. The goal when one talk this out loud and one reflects the person will honestly say they do not feel that way. The other thing a person can do is be reflective when a negative thought enters one's mind and think why the person feels this way. The person can reflect what this event can become a learning experience.

This author understands how frustrating trying to achieve weight loss. This author has at one time experienced the struggles to weight loss. For instance, this author for years has struggled with weight loss and eating the right foods. This author on weight loss has good days but has set into motion a set of goals and timelines to eradicate weight loss for a healthier lifestyle. This psychologist tried the slim shakes, the diet pills, and increases other supplements but the fact remains to lose the weight he must control his intake of food. Social media adds and people posting photos of being trimmed Products such as Slim Fast and Hydro Cut but she/he soon realized it is smaller portions and smaller bites to control weight. Social media has an impact on everyone's life including this author's weight loss. Social media flaws also include folk who profess their extraordinary wealth has guaranteed them happiness.

Looking on social media, such as Facebook and Instagram, there exists a plethora of "wanna be's" who profess in being a coach and an expert in turning people's lives around. Most of this lack the credentials to profess One downside are people tend to think of these quick rich schemes and then will post them on things such as YouTube to declare which the person states how they obtained their riches by social media. Many social media sites center in self-gratification and self-interest, lack empathy and are the representation of the standard social system. Analyzing the ads on Instagram illustrates how the merchants want people to buy compulsively with remorse. Here is where the problem lies people making decisions, not on sound judgment but impulsivity. Hard work and persistent pay off and are part of the change empowerment for individuals.

Chapter Four

The truth be known, most people have worked hard and gained wealth through persistence and failures. One should always be grateful for those who have more, part of the key to higher money. This therapist believes being able to help others as well without charging large sums of membership or organizational fees is a goal of many psychologists. These may not be the case in corporate America. Companies will induce people to join the sales group, but the person may find paying membership cost, and annuals dues as a way for the organization to get richer at the expense of the individual. Organizations such as Herbalife have individuals pay dues, and another example can be Costco. People return merchandise and receive a gift card. Analytical data illustrates most of the people will lose the map or in the case of membership will quit and move onto something else. In the same way, people will hire a coach and will at some point drop the coach before success in changing the negative thought to a positive impression.

Coaches are helpful for people, but this psychologist believes some people, in the coaching business, lack the skills to train or take advantage in people who are exhibit low self-esteem and are at many conferences, the person believes in controlling their lives. Some of these people are in search for the "right formula" in life to make them better leaders, higher self-esteem, and great lovers. This psychologist believes the coaching needs to come within the individual and not to look outward. Making changes in one's life requires reading, learning, and self-reflection. It is not the coach who can make the difference in one's life but the person 'mindset."

1. Clarify the overall objectives and metrics of the coaching program. Align expectations.
2. Introduce the coaching process with the Client and, if applicable learn about the Client's past experiences with coaching.
3. Identify the Client's personal and career vision, values, priorities, and hopes for coaching.
4. Co-create with the Client a language and tools that can be used to push beyond current capabilities and limitations.
5. Review 360 or other feedback with the Client and identify clear and specific goals and metrics. Two key focus areas are competencies for top performance in current role and skills for promotion to the next position.
6. Map out an initial plan to get from point A (the client's starting point) to point B (coaching goals and objectives). Create a draft Leadership Development Plan.
7. Arrange a meeting with the Client and the Client's manager(s) to present high-level discoveries from the 360 and draft of the coaching plan and to get input from the manager(s).
8. Facilitate the Manager-Client-Coach meeting and work with the Client to revise the Leadership Development Plan, if needed.
9. Conduct bi-weekly telephone and in-person coaching sessions with the Client. The Client sets the agenda for each coaching session based on coaching goals, Client needs, and situations that have occurred since the previous meeting.
10. Perform periodic informal process assessments with the Client — What's working? What's not working?
11. Finalize the coaching with formal written feedback reports – one who prepares and provides to the Client sharing assessment of the Client's progress and suggestions for future development.
12. Schedule 3-month and 6-month follow-up coaching sessions to assess the Client's progress in meeting his/her developmental goals and provide suggestions for maximizing the Client's efforts.

If a person wants a change in their life the person, one must develop a strategy. Dr. Jeff Kaplan discusses a plan for coaching success. This psychologist believes the approach is to follow a plan to get from point A to point B for success. People such as Jim Rohn has argued one needs to have an idea to succeed in life. This psychologist would agree as does Admiral William H McRaven it is the meticulous details such as making one's bed in the morning add up to success. Little information and the simplest mundane tasks can enhance people's empowerment by creating a feeling of accomplishment and self-worth. People tend to forget the mundane details and are willing to give up easily. Giving up should never be an option.

The goal is always to learn in failures and move forward. The goal in any situation is being genuine and learn from the mistake.

Further, admit to the error and move on. This psychologist sees the value in owning up from one's mistake. This psychologist will talk about an adverse event or a failure out of his mind. Taling the adverse event out of consciousness usually occurs by talking out loud to himself and moving forward. This psychologist learns to be persistence and always have, one's goal in sight. When this psychologist was little, he was sent back in kindergarten. He learns through the years quitting and failure is not an option. His old mindset it was OK to leave and try again. Stopping became a pattern in high school, college, and finally with his marriage. Like stated above one gets to the point in life when things changed from a should to a must when this occurred ownership occurred, and this person took full responsibility for his actions. As Admiral says, "Don't Ring the Bell." Ringing the Bell means one quits! Mental changes require things to go from should to musts.

Further, as Tony Robbins states, "Things turn from shoulds to "musts" My work as a psychologist observes people who struggle in mental wellness and positive thinking. This psychologist firmly believes as a mental healer, the route to a healthier and happy lifestyle lives within the individual and not necessarily with the aid of a personal trainer or personal behavioral coach. People go to conference after conference, trying to understand themselves, and looking for the "golden grail" of happiness. Happiness must seek and find, happiness exists within themselves. Jesus Christ says, "Seek, and One will find." The answer lies with oneself. Changes occur rapidly once the person agrees a difference is in order. Once one realizes there is a time for growth and is open to dispute, a positive reformation will occur.

For a lasting change, this psychologist believes, a person needs to hit "rock bottom" and be willing to make the changes in their life. What this psychologist means by "rock bottom" is the person who knows they must make a change in their life because what is working now is not working. The person is desperate and is wanting to try whatever and is willing to make the personal sacrifices in life to complete the needed changes. This psychologist observes people daily, and those who wish to change are open-minded and willing to try anything at this point in their life. A set of urgency has begun, and the person wants a change in life. Research has illustrated a high rate of people either quitting or lose interests in their new mental capabilities.

For example, in this age of fit and trim, one can see this play out on diet commercials on televisions depicting the person happy after losing the weight. Others are seeing dating sites, so many out there it can be very daunting, where the person can attract the person of their dreams. It is not the dating site which creates this but the individual who sets into motion the possibility and the openness in drawing the right person. The point here is how we bring our mental state, and this attracts like-minded people. The point this psychologist states regularly is people must be willing to accept who they are in the present and be prepared to be open to the possibilities. This psychologist observed people who needed to quick smoking to have a happy and healthier lifestyle but refuse to quit because of their "comfort zone." It all boils down to people's mindset. Change the mindset, and rapid change will occur. A person must be open to stepping out of their comfort zone as well to achieve success.

Mental blocks have to break down to increase success in life. Mental blocks, i.e., math as discussed above, can create a negative thought process. Discussed above in math purpose is of this work is to understand and break the bonds of mental blocks. These blocks are inhibiting for any individual, but the breakdown and understanding is a person can succeed without costing them copious amounts of money.

Few coaches lack the training and development to be actual coaches and because they express this because the person feels they can have an impact on people. The other reason it is good money if a person is good at training and development.

The problem there are not too many who are good at this, and those who enter the coaching profession must be aware of how their training and development can impair another individual. Organizations such as SIOP (Society Industrial and Organizational Professionals) and APA (American Psychological Association) where training and development occur for coaching, should be the norm for people entering this arena to help others. My guess if you were to ask individual coaches if they are members of these organizations the theory of this professional would not be many. These organizations help prepare people to help those who want to change in their life.

The goal for change focuses on the individual own unique perspective. This psychologist through his observations and work is learning what may work for one individual may not work for another. Each mind is single and has it's past, social status and g-factor (intelligence) have an impact on the individual's lifestyle. This psychologist often remembers the bible passage, "I knew you when you were in the womb." Everyone has their style (visual learner or oral learner), and each person learns uniquely. For example, left brain people learn a certain way as well as right brain people. The secret lies in determining your style. Though attending a seminar may give one the foundation to change, it will be the person's action, or lack of, which will create the change. Don't count on commercial ads or social media gurus to say they know the secret. The truth be known there is no secret it all in empowerment in change. No secret formula it depends on one's action for the person to change their lives. The three-step process this psychologist offers focuses on personal reflection, writing, and prioritizing what is necessary for the individual.

At the time of this writing, many corporations are entering the four billion a year market to get their share of the profits for health and wellness. People who are fit and trim are view as being happy and have more fulling lives. Being healthy and slim may not be the best for some people mentally because it changes their outer appearance but not their emotional state. Corporate America will tell people about many things which will make them happy and prosperous. But this is the wrong message and a poor choice to listen. Granted a healthy lifestyle, no drugs, and no smoking can lead to a longer life. Personal and unique lifestyle can have an impact on a person's life and depicted in many medical studies. The fact health and fitness is a big industry and the consumers tend to be Gen X and Millenials which the marketing companies fight for the corporate dollar.

A healthy change in a person's life does exist. Observing all the plethora of books on self-improvement which floods the book market today is staggering. For example, this author has at least thirty self-improvement books in his library collection, this does not count the Audible books, and all carry different approaches to happiness and well-being. Here any author including this psychologist offers their unique perspective in leadership, empowering, and self-esteem building. The point many writers make is their success story and their unique way how to succeed in life. Here again, learning is an individual perspective.

For example, this psychologist was terrible in math in high school. His grades were anywhere from an F to a C. This psychologist would study even between his lunch hours to get grams per mole! The point here once he entered graduate school and had to take a statistics class his final grade was a solid B. Upon reflection this psychologist, learned a mental block emerged. The thought process of his skills in math was flawed. The fact occurred to him that he was going to get the BEST grade because he did not want it to affect his G.P.A. The result this psychologist was able to unblock the negative, and he learned if he needed to determine a vital theory or concept, the goal is to study hard and if required get help. The change resulted in his purpose and his persistence to seek advice and understand theory and concepts.

This psychologist believes the foundation in happiness lies within the individual and not the collection of self-help books. Though he lends out his books if a person addresses anxiety or fear, the books offer the person a mechanism to overcome negative thoughts. Setting time aside to take into account fears and concerns so an individual can increase their empowerment. The plan for success is setting the time alone to put forth an action plan. Once the person has the goal to achieve the next step is to put the program into action. Personal empowerment comes from accepting where a person is in their life, good or bad, and is willing to make personal changes to live a happier and fuller life.

Many professional coaches will argue the road to change and success doesn't happen overnight. Keep in mind, this psychologist explains, the way to happiness is hard and can be a life-long journey. Here again, in this instant gratification society, the process does not occur over time. This psychologist sees people who will ask how long this process will take and his usual answer depends on the individual and not the psychologist. Growth and change occur when the individuals want it to happen not when the court has ordered the person into drug rehab. This rationale occurs because the person has no remorse because the system saw that they committed the wrong.

Growth occurs not from the success in life, but the lost opportunities and the failures in life. This psychologist learns more from his failures than his accomplishments. He has learned as he continues his uphill climb, to help others who are less fortunate, be positive always, and be humble. Leaders and coaches profess those who learn from their failures and are still persistent, in their achievements. Once a goal obtains the objective is to reach higher levels of happiness and success. Here the secret successful people are not happy all the time but know when they must be up to their A game.

What this author calls his A game is he reflects at the end of the day did he accomplish all he wanted and did the day add value to people around him. There are days and sometimes weeks that this psychologist struggles not only with the day but also with the week. The point here is always to feel one is moving forward in life. There will be days one will take a step back, and there are days one will take four steps forward, the goal here is to be reflective on both good days and bad days. The process of happiness does not come from social media or the high salary for an individual, people with high wages can be unhappy, but from the personal happiness value, it is very subjective and personable. The real test is the individual who confronts adversity and sees themselves willing to learn and ready to make a positive change.

Chapter Five

Three-Step Approach

The three-step approach is a concept and psychological framework which can work on any gender, race, or age. The empowerment framework is simple in the method. The plan requires to write and reflect and does need time set aside each day. The three-step process is a roadmap and will help an individual navigate positive thinking. An individual will increase their critical thinking skills, reflection skills, and willing to be open to changes within one's life. The crucial point is to engage the individual to grow and learn from the three-step process. As stated above part of the formula in success, is in keeping an open mind and the result results in negative emotions and thoughts will decrease, and that alone will improve the individual life. Be reflective and critical through changing process to continually reflect in positive thinking which can have the most significant change impact in one's life. The formula of success is to increase empowerment within you and create a level of change which will be proactive somewhat than the reactive. The other vital things are taking ownership of the individual's life.

The learning process can be slow or can be fast. Here again, in this project of love, the individual rather than a set of psychological guidelines enhance a personal need to follow. The approach here is Solution Focused Therapy which looks at the solutions rather than the problem. Positive Psychology Program website argues Solution-Focused

Brief Therapy (SFBT) is the therapist must discuss the issue to find the answer. In this case, the individual will write the problem and how to address the issue. SFBT does not dwell on every little detail, so the point is to write the question in the individual's daily book. This psychologist believes if the person is not comfortable with the process seeing a licensed psychologist is also highly recommended. The objective in SFBT will not dive into the individual's past to understand one's present state, but rather, one needs to look at the present while working in the future. This psychologist believes you cannot change the past nor change one change the future, so SFBT is a great approach. Likewise if one feels this may be a bit daunting or complex, this psychologist advises seeking professional help.

Notes taken from the Positive Psychology Program illustrates critical issues and foundational beliefs that the SFBT model uses the following assumptions:

- Change is constant AND certain
- Emphasis should be on what is changeable and possible
- Clients must want to change
- Clients are the experts in therapy and must develop their own goals
- Clients already have the resources and strengths to solve their problems
- Treatment is short-term
- The focus must be on the future – a client's history is not a vital part of this type of therapy (Counselling Directory, 2017)

The rationale for SFBT is an excellent tool for this three-step approach because the solution focuses on the individual and the present.

Those individuals who want a quick fix may not get lasting change while those who take a serious approach to this written SFBT can make an everlasting change in their overall success in life. Consequently, since this book focuses on the individual, results, there will be different for ween two people if both read the book at the same time. One may share their goals and objectives with their mate, but since the results and the solution is individualistic the results will be different.

The point many people failed to address, like anything in life, is no two people are the same. The discussion above focus on people's perception of others. People tend to compare themselves to others. This psychologist often believes what may work for one person may not work for another. For example, life struggles have a significant impact on people's mindset, especially between unfamiliar cultures and races. When people do not understand religion, the person tends to close their mind or addresses a flaw in the person's rational mind. The only way to honestly know another culture is to live within the culture or be a part of that race.

This psychologist does not believe any person is above the other and respect and love should exist between all with the hope of love, understanding and communicating. This author sees how this current political system is corrupt and dysfunctional; there is a lack of compassion and understanding. The trust between the two party's policy is evil because of it more about the party than helping the American public. He further believes the lack of moral and ethical leadership does not exist between the leaders of both parties and assumes a new purge of leadership should emerge.

Further not saying anyone is bad or good is not the correct concept either. This psychologist pontificates people either make good choices or bad. This line of thinking of options should use de-humanize a person in thinking the person is terrible. The goal of this three-step process is not to look at the bad in one's situation but the good. One key concept to remember before going to bed and rises in the morning are grateful for the day. Appreciative statements help start the day in a positive note and leaves to the universe open to the possibilities.

Additionally, gratefulness helps create the foundation for the three-step programs. It is the little things in life, being thankful in the morning, which adds up during the day. Remember the little things add up to the bigger things. Being grateful and present makes the day start in a positive note and creates the opportunity in a positive limelight.

This psychologist knows everything in life is subjective and the personal journey is in the eyes and ears of the individual. The goal when talking with people focuses on a Solution Focus Approach rather than a Behavior Approach solution. The person knows the behavior is impacting their lives henceforth the individual may need some sound framework in where the process heads in the future. The goal of this three-step project is to offer a foundation to guide the individual of any age to succeed in life. As stated above the three-step process knows age barriers. When this psychologist depicts the correct use of this framework, the person is happy with their experience and are willing to be proactive in the changes. As the person goes on later in life, the person will be able to make the changes, if needed.

The terminology for this three-step process will be not scholarly form but, in a way, any age or any level of education can read. Secondly, women and men think different so the process, as stated above, so the process is tailored to the individual so male and female should not affect the person inhibitions. Men, for the most part, tend to be more visually oriented and women tend to be more oral oriented, but in either case, the step process focuses on individuality rather than the clinical direction. The goal here as stated earlier is to create balance within one's mind and be able to do the reflection and critical thinking to complete this process. Competition is subjective as well, but the person will be able to notice a change in their behavior and the approach of a negative mindset.

Let's begin the journey.

Chapter Six

Three-Step Approach

The first thing this author has learned through the years is whatever one plans in life; the result is never the way the person envisions. Majority of the time the plans in life never goes the way the individuals wants, and then anxiety and chaos begin. For example, this author has worked hard to change his weight and his "poor graduate syndrome philosophy. First, the burden for this author has always been a challenge and uphill climb in the last several years. There are days of success, eating the right foods such as greens and low carb foods, and the days the crazing for McDonald's cheeseburger takes a fierce hold os Skyline chili. The goal here is first aware of the short-comings concerning fast-foods. Be mindful of the weak moments and to be able not to be hard on oneself when the person fails. One thing this psychologist does he plans a day of fast, some weeks good other still a work in progress.

This psychologist believes in part of this learning process is to grow from the failures and to move one's life forward. Controlling the mind from this day forward and explain to the conscious and sub-conscious things will be positive. Personal empowerment comes from managing and creating the possibilities in life which will enable the person for the success and failures. For example, this psychologist has heard it is the other person's fault because the person left the chocolate cake on the counter. Failures and success exist with the individual, not the only person. The point is as the clique says, man up for one's mistakes! Instead of being passive aggressive and blaming the other person to the chocolate cake on the counter believe the person will do much better the next time the cake is on the table and will just let the cake be there for someone else.

The emphasis should be a mistake made by the person eating the cake. For example, this author has set into motion not to eat anything after 8 pm. The fault in eating after 8 pm lies with the individual and not with the food. Hold oneself accountable. For instance, if this author is grouchy for the day, the goal is not to blame the day or a series of events which may have enhanced the grouchiness but take reflection responsibility and correct the behavior. Find the cause of the action; for instance, if this psychologist is crusty, it is because of the night before he did not get a lot of sleep. He will then blame the transgression on his lousy judgment; sometimes it has to do with work, in any case, the fault of his wrong choice. Misbehavior and sick days can be exceptional learning opportunities.

This psychologist sees the values in learning opportunities on days which are harmful, or behavior is below par. The best solution in any negative experiences is to ask what can this person learn from the situation. This psychologist, for example, had requested this when a job he created is getting is a negative or positive vibe for him on any given day. For instance, he has been friendships he had no business being in and had a business relationship with people he felt did not bring anything to help his practice. Usually, his instinct gives the signal and it is at this point reflection and learning will occur. The thing to do in any situation, be reflective and ask, does this create positive growth in my future? Another example, this psychologist, works out of a warehouse and lives out of the warehouse in the past, but a breaking point came when the warehouse is robbed by some folks who have a disregard of themselves or want to empower their own lives. Instead of sulking and blaming the situation on the environment he concluded if he wants a change in his surrounding he has to make the change, and this is not up to others. If the event is a negative, more and likely, the situation developed by a series of mistakes the individual has made.

This psychologist believes the best solution is to take responsibility and change the environment to a positive. As discussed above, taking full responsibility for the action is a step to change and empowerment.

Praise the good days as well and the bad days and make a statement' "what can I learn from this situation." This author transformation recently occurred in looking not at the negative of the situation but the positive!! As people, we tend to view the negative in situations and not think of the positive impact a situation can have in changing and empowering our lives. For example, this author uses the "poor graduate syndrome" when he sees a bill not paid or forgets to do something during the day. One of his weaknesses is looking at school debt. The issue for him is transforming the debt from graduate school to a positive transformation. Instead of seeing student debt as a hopelessness endeavor of debt abyss, the author examines what he can do to change the perspective from a negative to a positive. The solution the school debt will help the psychologist get a better job and the debt has to increase his critical thinking, and he can work on writing which he truly loves. The goal is to make positive and proactive changes. In other words, change the quantum physics in mind. Change the negative thoughts to positive thoughts.

For instance, this psychologist likes to read, and he has a few things published in the past. He enjoys speaking at conferences, and he enjoys engaging people. His English skills have been a troublesome foe since he enjoys writing. Instead of taking the approach that he is not a good writer and he should not write. His thought process is why not write more and the more he writes, the better his writing will become. In more significant projects such as this, he plans to have someone edit his grammar and the flow of the paper. The point here, it is easy to get discouraged and frustrated but to be in the arena and to fight is the best way

Once we can change a negative thought into a positive impression, the goal is to take responsibility for the change and ownership of the ideal. In other words, how can one change a thought process into a situation which is doable and containable rather than a feeling of hopelessness and out of control? Telling oneself, they are responsible for the problem, and it is their responsibility to solve the problem. Removing a negative starts the process of self-awareness and empowerment for the individual. Positive thinking emerges, and less stressful situations arise and increase self-awareness and increase one's thinking ability.

If one is sending negative thoughts to their brain waves, the mind becomes blurry, and the individual can not focus correctly. Specific food allergies can do this for the brain as well. For example, the author limits his intake of wheat. He has found more significant amounts of wheat intake like bread will fog his mind, so the input in wheat limits interaction with people and clients. Drinking alcohol or certain perspective drugs can have this effect on his as well. This psychologist like to be focused and centered on every detail he completes in his research and writings. Positive energy to the brain waves can destroy harmful brain waves and create clearer critical thinking

The mind works as well as what one is feeling at the time. This psychologist learns the mind is the leader in your emotions and your feelings. People who are leadership positions in a specific industry believe the person can be an excellent coach. Private coaching is a very professional field, and people think anyone can be a coach who is further from the truth. People assume with limited training, such as a certificate, they can have an impact on people's lives. This psychologist would agree some people are "born" to help others and can have a way of helping others to grow. This psychologist has seen on social media such as Instagram and YouTube in people who claim they are wealthy and can have an impact on changing another person. This psychologist sees this as a skeptical, but this psychologist argues empowerment and change are subjective. People have to be persistent and want change, and this psychologist sees that some leadership programs offer "A Quick Fix" and offer any other solutions to long-term situations.

As a psychologist, my readings and observations, this author see leadership coaches profess that the body and the mind need to align for transformation to occur. The brain, which is the mind, can achieve things far higher than a person can imagine. The potential for growth in memory is endless. People accomplish things through visualization and writing such as self-reflection. There are cases where the brain has healed the body. People will pay for diseases to disappear and there is no medical reason for the disappearance other than a miracle! People pray for healing, and it occurs, but the mind is an instrument for the cure. For example, people meditate and do yoga for mental and cleansing to occur. Research indicates athletics healing occurs faster with the correct mindset. Injuries which should have taken eight months to heal for an injured football player have taken place in 6 months span. The best approach is to keep a positive attitude and let the brain control the positive vibes. We create, and we attract what a person believes in one's mind.

Concerning the "Laws of Attraction," the mind attracts what a person feels and want through their existence in life. For instance, people set into motion wanting to get married or draw the right person to marry. Other people tend to settle when the person seems to think this person is for me and dates and hopes a bond of marriage will occur. As people, we attract people of the same mind. In other word, people draw want they believe for them whether the person is or not if the person has some form of mental blockages, such as low self-esteem or anxiety, the result the person attracts the wrong person in one's life. Ideally, people need to be whole and pure to draw the correct person in life. The person has to love themselves and feel free of any anxiety or fear. This psychologist believes one factor in the high divorce rate is people attract a person but once the attraction wears down people develop excuses on why they need a new partner because the person can not connect to their spouse or lover.

Here are why people need to be whole and pure with themselves before going back into the dating scene after a divorce. This psychologist observes people who are currently separated on dating sites and dating again. This psychologist believes there needs to be healing and reflection before moving on in life. Another situation that arises in this society of instant gratification people do not wait and always believe things will be greener on the other side. The grass is more ecological philosophy holds in a relationship where a person feels the love is gone or the connection not there. The mistake becomes a cyclical behavior and gives the impression as this psychologist professes the "ongoing gerbil wheel" of life. Either the person is married four or five times, does not understand the word committed relationship or has ethical or moral problems. The mind has to be in a decent and balanced place before any changes in life can occur.

This psychologist argues that changing the body is secondary to the mind. For changes to occur, one must change the mind first. The brain is the center of what we can achieve. For instance, concerning our health, the mind can play a pivotal role in how our health effects and can improve one's outlook. Action for the brain needs priority like exercise people have to feed the mind positive energy. Positive creates an action plan for the brain to remove a negative mindset and to restore the memory to its' proper alignment. Positive energy creates an affirmative action because if one has a negative mindset, this creates a negative response which in essence is no action or the no increase in self-empowerment.

When an individual needs to create an action, it should occur within seconds. This psychologist likes to use the five-second rule. For example, this psychologist uses the five-second government created by Mel Robbins. The base for this is an individual has five seconds and the thought overtaken by the conscious and the sub-conscious mind. If one does not react within five seconds changes are the ideal or the action will not occur. Once you do not act within five seconds, the brain will sabotage the idea. One must make swift action or the suggestion this transformation in the opinion is a great empowering tool. In most circumstances, because of fight or flight, in the early days of people, this was an excellent tool. In moderation, this tool can be a hindrance if one does not speak up in the meeting or does not go over and ask the person out.

To succeed one must act (proactively) in five seconds. This psychologist has learned this takes time and practice and would recommend reading the book as well. People ask what the outcome is of speaking out or asking the person out; this is trivial because the purpose is to ACT on the urge. As discussed above, this is part of the learning process, and the five-second rule is a tool to help one be boldened and more empowered in their life.

Further, some things increase the cognitive positive(quantum) interaction in the brain while others do not. The premise or the base is to change the energy in mind to a positive experience. Like this author has stated, improving harmful neutrons to positive takes some time and practice but can achieve over time.

The first step approach is natural, but it requires an individual to keep an open mind and reflect in their daily life in areas of improvement and areas that seem to be a struggle in life. The purpose of any empowerment program is to give the individual the tools for success. The first step in any process is a solid foundation. Once the foundation is a secure and robust success is much easier to accomplish. Remember success is very subjective and personable, so the goal in this step is open-minded and self-reflective. Progress should be n small steps but success is individual in the area of the person wants to change. For example, losing weight for someone can be a success, especially health issue while being the top salesperson in the firm is the success of another. Success measured by the individual's experiences and growth and the amount the person is willing to change. The objective is keeping the mind in a proactive state by filling the mind positive reformations rather than negative. Being positive can be challenging but can be very rewarding.

Keeping the mind in a specific state is a struggle and requires a lot of practice. A person has to be persistent and be willing to try different concepts. Negative thoughts can sometimes occur on an hourly basis, by programming in the correct way. The brain can stay in a positive state. In the three-step process, the first step, one must conquer is negative thoughts.

Negative thoughts removal is a daily and grueling commitment to achieving success. Negative thoughts removal occurs on those struggling days. There are days when sometimes removing negative thoughts occur hourly; even this author sees negative thoughts enter in his mind. He uses different techniques to eliminate negative thoughts by an exercise which he uses to expel the negative feelings like demons. The author plays a mental game good thinking versus lousy though. The game is a death match, with a wire cage. He envisions the certain idea slamming negative thought to the mat. My goal is always is to play with the negative thinking, and at times this author will even talk to the contrary opinion. The talking idea will argue with the negative impression and ask why the view feels this way? The goal here has a battle with the opposite view, and the winner is the removal.

In the past, these negative thoughts, this author referred to this psychologist negative demon which has caused hardships and has created distance with people I loved. Negative thoughts can devour your life if not controlled. Negative thoughts enhanced the mind by adding stress and anxiety to one's life. People run from their negative feelings, put them aside, or ignore them altogether. In each case, the negative thoughts add emotional and psychological baggage to their life. Everyone at some time or another has a used the three above or in a combination of-of one. To rid of the three-excuses, stay focused and take ownership and responsibility in your mistakes and failures.

Taking ownership is vital in any situation for growth and development. Many individuals will blame others or run from the position will never develop and grow. The goal to increase self-esteem is to take ownership of the problem and making the problem disappear over time. People see their problems and rather ignore them and think the issues go. In actually, the issues emerge more fierce because of the reluctance to addressssss the problem. The best thing on more significant ownership issues is to break the components in parts to solve. People see issues, when the problems are overwhelming, will also ignore the challenge. The goal here is again is break problems to working parts. For example, when this psychologist, started his P.h.D. program he needed to finish 63 credit classes. Examing the credits look daunting to the psychologist at the time, but he was able to break this by category by level. By the time he started the dissertation he had finished the class work. For daunting and enormous task break the secure task forms that fit the personal lifestyle.

Two years ago, when finishing scholarly articles on why people, namely Native Americans, have a feeling of hopelessness, this author, was in Arizona, one of my favorite states and took a walk and was reflective on his own life. In reflection, why at times things appear to be in a state of hopelessness, for this psychologist he began to understand his past and how he can make changes in his life. This author realized the feeling was just that a passion and for to correct life's mistakes change had to occur. Errors are part of the growing process in life, but the correct thing to do as an individual learns from their failures. Once the mistakes emerge then thee times is to let go of the error and move forward in life.

This author had to let everything go in the past. Realizing after my failed marriage in 2007 and trying to start a relationship soon after the wedding the relationship doomed from the beginning. The negative thoughts swarmed in mind like hurricane devouring any positive thinking which could emerge. With the failure of the link this psychologist reflected and decided he needed to withdraw and to figure his life and pull things together.

This psychologist firmly believes people exist in the image of God but as we're not perfect. Like the saying goes people are a work in progress. The author realizes mistakes add to one's personality. The goal for this psychologist is to learn from the mistake and move forward. Once a person makes a mistake and is remorseful and take ownership of the mistake healing begin immediately. This psychologist believes once we take ownership doors open which were close before and a transformation within the individual occurs. Taking ownership is part of being in the "Present" because of the person's commitment to change now.

This psychologist believes living in the "Present" rather than dwell in the past or look at the future. In both cases dwelling, in the past one can't do anything to change the outcome and its psychologist belief the person is wasting emotional energy and creating a channel for negative thoughts. The future on the hand is worrying or fretting over something that might or might not happen. Here again, this is a waste of emotional energy and creates a channel for negative thoughts. One can only change the present because the person is living in the present. The gift is a life changer for some people. Psychologists and coaches will say only live in the "present" because you cannot do anything only regret and anxieties. Living in the here and now is what this psychologist calls a reformation in mind! The mind thinks of the things in the present and does not dwell in the future or past.

Secondly, living in the "Present" creates a more genuine person than someone who is thinking about the past or the future. For example, when people start a conversation with other people, the person can have an impact on the validation in communicating with the person. People tend towards thinking during the interview rather than listening to what the person is saying. The person is thinking, about what they are going to say or dwell on the discussion from yesterday; for example, the communication is fermented and flawed. This psychologist sees this as well when people are yelling and screaming. Arguments are the first negative thinking pr, the process of thinking of the past. People who live in the present and genuine tend to be more open in their communication and are present in their conversation. Further, people who have to be sincere and honest to themselves before being honest and real to others. People tend to create drama by not being authentic, and the person can tell the person is not engaging in the conversation.

As a psychologist, if this author is going to help others, which he felt God is calling him to do this so the individuals can profess a change in their positive life. This process of evolution occurs when people are genuine and sincere. For example, in the past, this psychologist mental devil would take hold of his mind. Instead of being real and authentic this author would interact with people by "Bull Shitting" his way in many situations and conversations. Upon deeper reflection, this is a tool this author learned at the age of five to six years old.

Reckless behavior like good behavior can damage a positive mind. Once a harmful habit forms in the brain, it takes a while for those bad habits to turn into positive reformations. This author 's thoughts had achieved some unruly behavior through this process, due to the fear and rejection in love from others, this infected his mental wiring as unfavorable. Remember the objective is to change negative behavior to positive behavior.

The author would say he was sorry but would repeat the same negative behavior. B.F Skinner states to change a negative behavior one must have to find the power of the source in the adverse action. Saying sorry made me feel the behavior change, but it did not. Saying sorry was like getting drunk, just gave this person a temporary high. Mentally my negative behavior was a quick way out of the situation without any remorse. To remove the harmful poison, in such a way that a person this person to be sorrowful and responsible for the behavior. In the same way, this psychologist does not drink anymore, soul searching and forgiving my past has led to a healthy positive mindset.

This process has been over 40 years in the making, and part of the problem is to reach "rock bottom" and realize the pain and acceptance of a change to "must" needs to occur to make a permanent change. This "rock bottom" must occur in life for a chance to develop because without wanting a change the unruly behavior will continue. "Rock Bottom" is seen in people who with a DUI, lose driving privileges and their healthy life, in the person's eyes, is disrupted. The majority of people REGRET that the person was found and not necessarily wanted to change their life. Or those in drug rehab who join a support group chances are the person will suffer a relapse because the person is not remorseful or will accept responsibility. People want to change in their life but do not know at times how about changing. The necessary foundation is family and friends.

Change in one's life opens new avenues for growth and empowerment. Creating the exact positive change can offer an open in the reformation and can help one assess the value in friendships, loves one, and family members. Focusing on people who can enhance one's growth is an additional success in a positive mindset. As discussed above, past barriers can create problems; the goal is always to surround oneself with people who help one achieve their goals in life — seeing people who hit "rock bottom" may at times be a good thing since the person will be forced to change their lives and does not like the feel they any more.

The discussion so far is centered on a negative mindset. Negative people around someone can have an impact on their positive thoughts. A person has to be aware of those around them, and the effect of the people have on their outlook in life. Having positive people around oneself is the key to healthy growth. There is an old clique, pick your friends wisely. Having people who are unhealthy is not suitable for your vibrations or one's sanity. One has to have the correct people in their circle of influence. This psychologist prefers to have an inner ring and an outer loop of influential people who he can depend on to get him through the difficult times in life.

This psychologist sees an inner circle consisting of no more than five people while the outer-circle can be no more than twenty people. The key is having the right people within the individual's lives. For example, this psychologist, have people with a least a four-year degree, he tends to have more female in his outer circle than men but here again depends on the subjectivity of the individual. The key is to have people who can influence his life and have a positive impact on their life. Family and relatives are excluded from this list because relatives are in a category of support system. This psychologist believes the goal in life is to find people who will bring out the best in the individual.

The inner circle, are the people who are the closest to the person and has the most significant influence. Jim Rohn states, the person personality consist of the average of the five closest people to them. If any these people are negative, this will have an impact on one 's life. People have to be supportive in this empowerment change and for that matter life in general. This psychologist argues that a robust support system crucial for growth and prosperity.

The discussion on mentors and coaches is pivotal in life. This psychologist uses mentors and coaching to enhance his career as a psychologist. He uses mentors in the use of professionals field as well and has a couple of people he uses as mentors to increase h, is knowledge and his professionalism. The goal for any person is to remove negative thoughts and create a more peaceful and positive lifestyle.

The three-step approach can and will change one's behavior. There are many approaches to leadership, self-esteem, and motivation currently on the book market. Many personal coaches and see acclaimed guru authors discuss how to change behavior, and to how to make positive changes, in one's life. GThe message focuses on the unpleasant habits which impact people lives. The rule and results are changing the behavior to a positive reaction. This psychologist believes all people in life want and needs positive habits. The problem emerges when people are stuck or do not know how to remove the bad habit.

Research indicates that many people fail or give up in changing unruly behavior due to proper follow-up and or the commitment by the individual. The adverse reaction is seen by how many people drop out of the gym by March or April. Another example is those who smoke or drink too much and feel a sense of hopelessness in changing their lives. The person continues to drink and smoke until the effects take a toll on the person body. This author sees people go to their grave because of lack of will power. For instance, people who need to give up smoking continue to smoke. This therapist believes people need to reach out to others for help and guidance with the correct professionals who can help change hopelessness around.

This psychologist believes a lot of self-help coaches use a general format rather than create a program for the individual. The issues for many coaches is the cost factor and the time factor. The approach many coaches use is quantity rather than quality. One-on-one coaching is time-consuming. One reason is this would be an excessive cost to the customer. Coaching one-on-one is most effective because everyone's brain is individualistic and the mind and the electro-wiring is very subjective to the person. In essence, coaches try to put a square in a round hole by creating a program based on research and the overall results of the study in a general population. Coaching is why a mentor can make the difference within an individual and can create new growth for the individual. This psychologist sees the value of individuality and catering the results to the individual will create a positive change which creates a positive individualistic transformation in their life.

As stated above, the attempt is a proper engaging technique will engage the individual to create a change in their life. The discussion focuses on negative behavior or negative thought. The object is to take the negative and make the behavior or thought into a positive. With this first hurdle in life meet any other feelings of hopelessness can easily be transformed into a positive experience which can help the individual better cope with life's challenges. If one life can change through the process from this work or study, it is privileged writing this work.

For example, this psychologist goal is to write five-pages a night. The goal is the long-term where he likes to see the finished product of this work. Though the three-step is not the panacea or a cure-all approach for individuals, the three-steps can offer a road map in achieving greater happiness. The goal in every step is to reflect on each level and making notes through the process of reading this work. Reflection brings about nightly healing and positive reformation. Meditation is best at night and in the morning when there are no distractions. Writing this has been very therapeutic for the author and has led to many serious reflections. Reading and meditation is part of the growing process and is a good indication of achieving real goals in life.

For example, when this psychologist reads a new concept or a unique leadership style he makes copious notes and uses his nearby color markers on point he agrees or disagrees. He would further write down things he enjoyed and learned about the book or journal article. The rationale behind this is he will make notes or markings and will go back and review. Just like the signs and the markers the brain is doing the same function. Marking down things the mind enjoys and things the spirit does not possess. The negative thoughts and patterns need to be removed from the brain while the positive experiences need solidification to the brain. Killing the wild thought waves and replacing them with positive thought waves increase health and happiness.

Throughout this book, the mind is capable of change, but the difference is subjective to the individual. A person has to be open to the switch and is willing to create the possibility of turn. This book is a work on thoughtful suggestions and the psychologist own personal experiences and observations. The best advice from this book is to learn from what one sees the most value in their own life. Here again, this is subjective. This psychologist never likes to argue with people and has compassion even to strangers. The rationale, unless the person knows about the other person, who never knows what the other person day is like or what a person is going through at the time.

For example, at this time of this work, the author's dad is in full leukemia, he is finishing his research, and has made a commitment to a publisher concerning this book. Additionally, he is the divorced dad of three teenage girls, looking at moving to Tucson Arizona, and wanting to spend time with his BFF who is 1754 miles away in Arizona. Additionally, he has to work full time to pay his bills and provide for his girls. In summary, this psychologist at present has a pretty full plate and recently got over a nasty head cold which threw his plans a week behind schedule. If you did not know this psychologist and ask me to attend an event or go to a party, the quick response would be no. The psychologist means the did not want to go but at the moment priorities and boundaries are in place in his life.

With this said, this is why this psychologist tends to listen and observe things before commenting or offering a professional opinion. This therapist believes in an open mind and seeing how people react and watch their eyes as a key to excellent listening skills. He has worked with business and has worked with a small company which he helps advice on people they need to hire.

Working with people in small business and larger businesses, this psychologist sees no use in working with people who mind is close and not willing to grow. Additionally, people who often recommend reading the material but the person refuses or neglect the reading material usually can be seen as close-minded. Here again, this psychologist taught at the junior-college level and preferred students who wanted to learn and were open-minded. This psychologist admires educators because, especially K through 12 grades, because students may not be necessarily there to learn and the teacher is forced to engage the student. Younger students are not close-minded; they lack the skills of proper learning.

Close-minded individuals, tend to be a bit pessimistic about their life and tend to have a sense of hopelessness about their future. This psychologist does not even have to engage with these people; sometimes one can see this in the way the person walks or in their facial expressions. Many are slump over, slow talk, and the eyes are to the ground. Additionally, facial expressions show the lack of positive activity to the face and the person seems to be stressed or frown in the front. Many do not live in the present, and many dwell in their past. The key here for people is to be open to the possibility in life and be open minded to the change in their life. Be proactive and be willing to keep an open mind in the three-step approach.

Being proactive means taking a look at situations in life and willing to meet them head-on rather than be reactive and adjust to them after the condition occurs in one's life. The more proactive a person is in their life, the more the person is in charge of their life. Reactive people tend to be depressed, or low-self esteem, passive-aggressive, and instead blame someone else on their lack of action. Responsive people let the day run them while proactive people are the opposite. Do receptive people see the negative things as why me while the dynamic person depicts what this event can teach me? It all about learning and being active in life.

Further, this book focuses on people expanding their lifetime learning. This psychologist is a lifetime learner. He would also classify himself as Renaissance Man. The term does not mean a person who lived in the Renaissance but rather a person, male or female, who is talented at many different things, no matter the time frame of the person who lived. Some of the characteristics of a Renaissance man are master of many fields of work, charming, witty, well-educated, athletic, well-mannered, and self-controlled.

Examples are Albert Schweitzer in the twentieth-century was a theologian, musician, philosopher, and doctor. And Benjamin Franklin who was an author, printer, politician, scientist, inventor, and soldiers. Franklin founded the first public library as well. Another one is Thomas Jefferson who was a brilliant scholar, inventor, naturalist, and architect, Thomas Jefferson played the violin, spoke six languages, conducted archeological investigations of Native American mounds, founded the University of Virginia, and assembled a 10,000-book library. He forms the foundation of the Library of Congress. Another example, a female model is Margaret Higgins Sanger, taken from Wikipedia, she was an American birth control activist, sex educator, writer, and nurse. Sanger popularized the term "birth control," opened the first birth control clinic in the United States, and established organizations that evolved into the Planned Parenthood Federation of America. All the above had a passion for learning and helping those who were of less fortunate.

Further, lifetime learners tend to be people who keep an open mind and are willing to learn. Part of this lifetime learning focuses on personal education for themselves. Looking at the bad behavior is not the solution but looking at how to change the resolution is a better approach. One of the paths many psychologists use is the clinical base approach. This psychologist likes to use the Solution Based Focused Therapy which focuses on the solution of the problem than on the bad individualistic behavior. This solution focus is centered on learning or engaging the individual in the behavioral process.

The objective of this book, as discussed above, focuses on the individual. Part of individual behavior is the wrong approach to lifetime learning which focuses on the individual and his/her value in education. The process of engaging the individual learner is part of positive thinking. Empowerment comes from the individual in taking ownership of their knowledge and empowering the learner. Educators also use this approach of engaging the learner. Like learning lifetime learner should be fun and seen as an adventure. The reason this psychologist bases this three-step approach of the Solution Based Focused Therapy (SBFT) for this exercise because the solution is not what is wrong but more on how to make the right choice in life.

People tell a story of what is wrong with them when in some cases it may not be what's wrong with them but what choices a person makes in life. SBFT does not look at the behavior but the individual and ask what can be imaged in their life to make a difference. The results focus on the outcome of the new act the individual inspires.

Part of the three-step process is setting aside time to read and reflective. A person should set aside forty-five minutes a day to read. The reading list is something out of the comfort zone and a reading list of leadership, self-esteem, and empowering oneself or others. This therapist professes in removing negative thoughts and create positive brain networks to the mind. The problem for many these days people spend less time reading and when reading pick articles which read at a six or seventh grade level. The purpose is to grow one's mind and to grow in positive thinking.

The concept in this book is the process of learning which involves reading on a daily bases. Reading creates a positive environment in the brain and generates growth in brain cell activity. An example, this psychologist likes, is to view is the books that Bill Gates recommend in reading. He sees Gates book's as a way to future his perspective about issues. He also likes to see the book list of Warren Buffet as well. Many leadership coaches, such as Tony Robbins are Bibliophile readers. For example, this author reads a least a book a week and always ask friends and family in what they are reading currently.

One person he admired greatly was Teddy Roosevelt who was an avid reader. Reading needs to be fun and adventurous. Teach children early how to read. Earlier children reading depicts how children can succeed in school and life. The purpose here is not to read a book a week but if one is not reading now to find a book which can engage the person to expand their knowledge. This psychologist would argue against starting slowly in your reading selection and then work up slowly and pick another book one finds entertaining. Read to have fun and enjoy!

Another thing to keep in mind in this book is the process to be optimistic and enthusiastic in your approach in this reading. This psychologist often asks how he maintains a positive outlook and an enthusiastic attitude to life. The basic answer what is the alternative to be pessimistic and pollute the mind with negative thoughts and unhappiness. Secondly, he reads books and journal articles which expands his world and knowledge of events in his life. His goal also is to read the material in which he will learn a new theory or concepts concerning something he is studying currently. Reading opens the door to new learning and forms positive learning environments. The option of being positive creates opportunities which otherwise, would be negative thoughts. If one is open-minded and creates the possibility, things seem to fall into place in life.

The three-step approach will be reflective of the triggers mechanisms of negative thoughts in mind. For this author, he plays a game with his mind where he can go 24-hours without a negative thought in his mind. Playing a mind game is quite tricky because this psychologist has at present many situations around him, people he knows, who are in some crisis mode. Negavity exhumes every pore of their body and is out of control in handling their negative environment. Mind games are a complicated process to remove negative thoughts within 24 hours. This psychologist tries to block off time to control an unfavorable opinion and for this psychologist, this process can be at times a minute by little pain n his mind. He sees a certain idea as a unique approach when the mental demon enters his mind. One strategy he does is this psychologist plays a game where the images the worse and then laughs about the process. Chances are one 's thoughts, and the results are not always as worse. This psychologist believes and sees the results are somewhere in the middle.

People would debate being over-positive is a bad thing? An individual through ta his process of the book needs to make sound and rational judgments in goals and objectives she/he can achieve. Overachieving is a useful skill, but the balance in stress and emotions must stay in balance. Unbalance in life can add weight and other emotional disorders for a person. The objective of any solution is to be within the range of one's goals. People try to achieve outside the normal goal range, and others will overshoot their targets. The goal objective should be reachable with the help of a mentor or even a coach who can shed their perspective in reaching one's goals. This psychologist believes if an individual achieves the intent that she/he aspired this will empower the individuals and creates a sense of self-worth and self-esteem.

Empathy will also increase which is the feeling of helping of others. Compassion understands the opinions of the other individual. Research as showed people who have tremendous insight are excellent leaders. Leaders who can motivate others are in high demand because for the most part people instead follow than lead. Through the observations of this psychologist, followers tend not to like conflicts and more in tuned to themselves, but leaders tend to see the 'bigger picture' in things somewhat the specifics and energized by battles if the disputes are part of the final results. Leaders tend to be proactive while followers tend to be reactive.

A final thought about being proactive is a person who wants to increase their empowerment needs to try to be active for a week. The individual will see a vast difference in their la life. Part of being productive is to be reflective and meditative. The individual needs to find what works in one's growth and what does not work in this proactive approach to increase their empowerment. This psychologist has learned through his learnings and dealings with people; it is best to listen to others opinions and try to comprehend what the individual is saying or what is this person teaching at this present time. For example, people seem to lack excellent listening skills, and examples of poor listening exist in and out of the work environment. A program which creates effective listening skills is 360-degree feedback. A brief introduction of this method discussed above.

360-degree feedback goes by names as well multi-source assessment, multi-rater feedback, and multi-source feedback is a process where feedback from an employee's subordinates, supervisor, colleagues, and self-evaluation by, the employee themselves. The information is gathered and shared with the individual. Self-reviews are another. Start aa existing listening skills. Believe in one's strengths and weaknesses.

Researchers have argued on working on one's strengths and weaknesses. Which approach to work on first is subjective to the individual. This author believes use is examining strengths if this is the one is the most comfortable. Try both strengths and weaknesses and find which is most effective in analyzing. The approach works best. The goal to remember is to look at which will have the most significant impact to change one's life. This psychologist believes, As stated above, strengths and weaknesses are subjective, and the only way to improve is the person wants to change.

This psychologist sees people who come to him, and state they have made changes, upon further analyzes what the person sees as a replacement is nothing more than the same behavior viewed differently. People say their going to church and are a new person but once their out of their 'new comfort zone" a way they are coping with anger issues, the change is limited if nonexistence. The change occurs because things are a must in life. The permanent change has to become a new habit and depending on the individual. Changes in behavior can be four to six weeks and in some cases longer. In the three-step process, what works for the person concerning anger issues may not necessarily work to make to change on the next individual. The foundation of knowing one's strengths and weaknesses can enhance the must, and through the process of analyzing one's strengths that is great if wish to choose weaknesses, this is great as well. There is a clique. "It's all good." The goal is steady and stable reflecting on creating massive empowerment and change.

The step is goal reflecting. Setting a goal is the first step is to be reflective; this forces yourself to set reasonable goals but also, reflect on the goals daily or weekly. In either case, one has to be thoughtful. This psychologist will even write pros and cons on 3 x 5 cards to clarify things. The objective is to have written out goals and daily weekly and monthly goals. Vague goals or lack of goals period can distract and set one on a course one had no intention. This psychologist always envisions in his mind a boat with a sail. A ship without a sail drifts to oblivion. Many people go through life without accessing their goals and objectives and see the value of immediate gratification such as name recognition or satisfying one's ego. Ego is very subjective but needs to be petted and cared to maintain.

This author had a friend ask me a while ago, why politics is not a part of his life as it was in my 20's and 30's. Upon future reflection, this author found this stroked his Ego but did not create profound healing. The politics were something he tried and to be honest towards the end of the 2000s became bored and disinterested. This author was not being genuine with himself, which led to the destruction and the abyss of his life in his 40s. Consequently, these poor choices in his 30's and 40 's have taken a decade to overcome. The positive mindset is not to remember the past but to look at the present. The destruction in self-narcissistic behavior and instant gratification led to poor goal choices and dead-end results. Part of the problem was always running and taking on the responsibilities of his action. The goal was to stop running and take responsibility for personal effects and to create solutions. Taking responsibility is a significant upward hill battle he plans to conquer. The first step is a mindset! Then the second is the person to take on the responsibility of their action.

A mindset may vary from time to time as well. There are up and downs in people's mind. There is also low, and high energy levels but the person has to be aware of the mindsets. Like life, in general, there are decisive moments, and there are negative moments. The goal and the purpose in life are to learn from the experience and move forward. For example, this author often sees people in professions who may serve in some other business. Psychologist and researchers depict people will change their job at least three to four times in their lifetime. The reason is their mindset sees that the person respect or feels they can get better pay elsewhere.

The mind attracts negative distractions. If one has a negative thought it is like a magnet to metal, the negativity holds on and will not let, go. The confident person is the less likely she/he will say attractive negative thought. All individuals have negative thoughts the issues is how can we control those negative thoughts and make the outcome a success. People who are confident and focused are more likely to see a change occur. A confident and empowered individual is a person who is aware of her/his short-comings and is proactive to make the change. The person has a high level of self-awareness and can act according. This psychologist sees this in people meditating in the morning and or evening to get their focus on what works for the day and how to improve their day by being more positive.

People have short-comings and as this psychologist agrees there are times of failure. Researchers and coaches argue it is the individual who makes the correct decision to move past the defeat and move their life forward. It is what the person does or does not do with the crash and to change the negative mindset which can make a difference in their lives. For example, a person who keeps working on getting the job of their dreams holds a positive approach and is willing to learn from their mistakes. People often here how actress and actors go out numerous times for a role aa and meet objections. For example, Mark

Ruffalo's meeting with Kenneth Lonergan must have seemed like a once-in-a-lifetime chance. After all, Ruffalo claimed in an interview with Moviemaker magazine that he had appeared in 800 auditions before Ruffalo managed to find the sort of the success that he wanted, which speaks well of his perseverance when it comes to his ambitions if nothing else. Winston Church gave a commencement which he told the audience never give up. Most success and positive people think of ways to win.

This psychologist believes a win is an authentic component of a positive person. The action defines success in life changes the life of the person for the better. The Men's Journal discusses fifteen ways to; win at life: Factors and traits that help people thrive

1. Optimism
2. Spirituality or religious belief
3. Motivation
4. A proactive approach
5. Eagerness to learn
6. Flexibility
7. Adaptability
8. Social competency
9. High self-esteem
10. Finding opportunities to succeed
11. Support from employers/family/community
12. Manageable challenges and difficulties
13. Calm environment
14. "Self-rule," which is like self-control
15. Skills

The real test of character is a person who creates a win/win/ for themselves. A win/win concept can increase the caring, empathy, of the person within his inner circle. The goal is not to win at another person expense. This approach is a negative situation because the person is taking advantage of another person. The goal here is to share the win with those people who one loves and to share the gratitude with oneself and those around their inner and outer circle. People who are grateful and illustrate appreciation throughout the day create new empowerment for themselves and others around them. One has to be thankful for the people in their life. An empowered person reflects in those in his outer and inner circle as part of this grateful feeling and those people who offer a positive influence.

People who are empowered must be aware of their surroundings. This psychologist perceives how one wrong individual within one's peer group can influence a person's positive behavior. For example, if a person is conceived to be a negative influence for this psychologist, he will not allow the individual to enter his sphere of influence. Additionally watching reality shows illustrates how certain celebrities allow people with flaws within their inner circle and the result is chaos and drama. Choosing friends is critical for success in life and that of any person who wants to empower their experience at a higher level. The key to any sphere of influence is to choose one's friends wisely. This psychologist ask does this person help or hinder my personal growth. Admiral McRaven, at commencement in Texas, focused on finding someone who will help you paddle in life. Find people who will support the decisions one makes in life and will be there when they need to paddle. This author uses a clique when he talks to friends about a specific situation. This psychologist will tell the person that he has their back!

This psychologist believes this happened when we chose a partner in life. People have a sense of love and trust for the people in which they love. The problem occurs when one or the one her person loses confidence. The phrase the "person has my back" is in jeopardy. This psychologist made a mistake in the past by dating someone that is not his type to date. He needed to attract someone to develop a loving and committed relationship. The person he dated he knew there would be no commitment. The problem occurs when as people we pick poorly. Dating and being with the right person is part of the result with whos is in one's inner circle. The other type of person is never comfortable being alone and has someone in their life throughout their life. Eventually, she/he figures they are not in a committed relationship and the person moves on but in actuality, have wasted time when she/he could have been in a loving and committed relationship.

This type of people is known as serial daters or as this psychologist believes the person is in a continuing relationship breaker. This therapist believes once the time comes to move on in life, the person begins to blame the relationship on the person rather than the other person. The passive aggressor blames the fault in the person. The problem occurs if a person commits to a soul searching exercise, the person dumped realized in the first place, that this person was not the one for them. In essence, the person made a wrong choice. This dilemma adds not only drama to one's life but also the negativity of not dating the correct decision. People who are in a loving and caring relationship will empower each other and support the other if the person can become a better mate. The right mate scenario occurs as well if one believes a "perfect body" will attract a "perfect mate." The statement is a flaw; people are attracted to the inner soul and the personality of a person so the wrong mate will lead to additional negativity. The change in physical appearances focuses on changing the person and having the person create a change in themselves.

A physical change can be a bit overwhelming for some who are in search of the "perfect body." Some believe if the person has a perfect body the person can attract the ideal mate. Physical attraction as the only factor in choosing a mate can lead to a broken relationship. Once the charm is gone, people make a disconnect in trust and not sure this person is genuine and sincere. Doubt occurs because the person whose body is going through a reformation needs to be aware of the change is physical. People change the outer appearance but neglect the inner-self such as emotional or spiritual renew. The person has a high value on external appearance but lacks the emotional or mental growth. Visible presence can be a factor in negativity in mind but a positive expression from the outside. These people believe in too much value on outward appearances and in some cases lack the social or communicative skills in life. Compare and contrast occur in these people and the consequences in a negative mindset. One needs to only compare themselves to themselves and not to others.

Those who are regularly using social media to boost their egos are not making the correct connection with their emotional self. Egos can play havoc in the negativity of the brain. Here again, the person compares themselves to other people. This psychologist recommends putting the cell phone aside and limits the time on social media. The problem which occurs concerns the disconnect of people. The person gives an outward positive impression, but there is something more sinister within the sub-conscious mind. Instagram and Facebook, for example, people will steal photos and profiles to portray to be someone else. Here people are not genuine with themselves and create a disconnect with other people. The result in both cases discussed above is inflated egos which can be deadly. The point here is to keep the ego in check and stress levels to a minimum.

The brain allocates for a certain stress level. Stress levels at level one are reasonable and can be a benefit for a person to stay focused. When stress levels achieve above level one and get into the two and three e levels people tend to lose focus and anxiety or depression can set in. The higher the stress level creates tension which creates a lack of sleep and a short temper. For example, those who cram for a test the next day or write a term paper at the last moment. Can lose focus in the exam and may make minor mistakes rather than prepare currently. The over-nighter creates a high level of stress and the term as well "all-nighters" lead to anxiety and a negative mindset which is not suitable for positive brain waves. Keeping stress levels low and proper planning of the day creates positive neutrons waves. Create and plan a positive work environment.

Having a positive work environment enhances the change in a positive mindset. People who let the job capture them before even walking in the door cannot have balance in their lives. My observations illustrate people lose focus at work due to the cell phone or social media. For example, when this psychologist needs to complete an important task, he will put the cell-phone on plane mode and awards himself when a mission complete. Doing steady writing for about fifty minutes in one given secession is the maximum he can do to complete success. He has learned that distractions kill positive energy and brain waves.

This psychologist argues the key to success is to stay focused on the task at hand. Additionally, he writes the goals agenda for the day on a 3x5 card when he wants to work on his book and how much time allocated.

This psychologist spends about 30 minutes at the end of the day reflecting on the success and failures of the day. Remember part of the three-step process is a reflection and analyzing the day. The proper thing for most people is to plan your day the night before going to work. Planning may be an impossible task because of time constraints, but he writes concepts or ideas he feels are essential tasks which need his urgent action the following day. This psychologist writes necessary vital plans or critical goals the night before work.

Here again, the goal and the reflection is the "best time" for the individual. For example, some people like to rise before dawn, say 5 am and feel they can accomplish much. Others, like myself, write better later at night when the energy flows. He has his coconut water and writing music which enhances his writing ability. Others may need quiet time and a cup of their favorite java. Reflection time is subjective, and the person has to find the "positive karma" which works best in their approach. The positive energy in the brain creates focus and clarity.

Reflection helps the positive brain waves and creates a higher focus on one's positive thoughts throughout the day. In the case a person has a bump in the day, they can solve the event quickly and move on with the rest of the day. It is not a hundred percent guarantee, but one will not have their day taken hostage. Hostage days by people in your circle or events at work or home do occur, but if the person is reflective and writes the reactions of the day, this becomes a learning opportunity. Observations by this psychologist illustrate people how many distractions happen, and people bombard one's day as soon as they walk in the door to work, home, or even on vacation. The goal in any of this is to observe keenly and to learn. A day needs a plan even when the person is physically wiped out, and their negative energy is high. As stated above, also a proper procedure has a 95% chance to end in some form of chaos.

For example, when a person plans a trip and they plan to see Hoover Dam; and the Grand Canyon. First, the trip plan in early March, but a freak snowstorm hits the Grand Canyon the day you arrive at the Tucson Arizona airport. The outcome and the thought process would be a negative outlook. How can this happen to me? The correct response will be what activities can the group see in Southern Arizona. The positive outlook would be to see the additional days sightseeing in Southern Arizona and a trip to Tubac and Bisbee. Both places highly recommended by this author. In other words, people have to create a positive thought for chaos which may or may not occur. Part of the learning process of the three-step approach is to keep an open mind and positive thoughts.

The three-step approach is enhanced by writing suggestions, feelings, goals, worries, and accomplishments down within a journal or even on a small notebook. One can keep in the journal nearby, or one can use the computer to write their daily diary. In any case, the idea is to write the things which come to the mind. The plans need to be clearly understood by the person. The goal is to write stuff in pure form. Write down things which go to one's mind. The goal is to write positive things rather than write down negative thoughts or ideas. For example, I own an ice cream delivery business, so this a goal I wrote for beginning the week:

I am always going to take things slower with all people this week and try to get more genuine and sincerer. I am also planning to do some reading this week and plan to take my one book to work this week. I also must be a beast all this week and must do ice cream as well. I see things as positive and will be positive around others as well. My goal is to make $1000 this week, and I am sticking to this goal.

Remember ideals and thoughts are in sub-conscious and will emerge. Writing the things down and seeing the thoughts create an action plan and the resolve to accomplish. Some times things come in the middle of the night. This researcher has received excellent ideas while fast asleep. This researcher thinks or recalls an excellent point once he gets up in the morning or writes it down immediately. He will achieve a pen and paper and write it down even if he is asleep.

For the three-step approach writing things down helps solidify one's day and create positive empowerment and energy. Remember keeps the list concise and straightforward. Writing big files is counter-productive, except for the grocery store; the goal is the simpler, the better. This psychologist recommends no more than five but no less than two.

This psychologist recommends writing no more than three things at one time. If one writes down three words, they need to accomplish through the day, the mind and the positive thinking will flow to the brain. A small pad of paper, with three essential tasks to achieve, is a way to empower the mind and create positive quantum energy in the brain. Additionally, this creates a real focusing technique. Once the first's day is complete, adjust for the rest of the week because this may be one's first attempt at writing. Once the person develops their unique pattern and perspective, one should feel the positive karma, and the positive energy will flow, and the negative energy will subside. Writing down takes practices and exploring what method works best for the individual such as calendars.

This psychologist uses a multi-calendar system. He uses a desk calendar and a calendar on his phone. The timing or technique needs to work for the individual. Calenders is a trial and error and what may work one week may not necessarily work the following week. One has to find the right combination to create the best positive energy and empowerment. For example, certain weeks work best for me such as a calendar on my desk. The following week it maybe is my google calendar the next week. Since he is entering part of the spring season which is his most busy season for his organization, he tends to use the Google Calendar on the phone because the phone will remind him of an important meeting.

This psychologist likes to write the event on his calendar on his desk and the phone. His mental process believes if one sees it since he is more visual than oral, then the task will be embedded in his mind. More than once memory will occur. For example, this author uses Google Calendar, 3x5 cards, and a desk calendar to write the day and weekly goals. The 3x5 tickets are for phone calls, and the Google Calendar is on my phone and alerts me the day before and two hours before the event. This way the author oversees his day rather than the day manages him. This psychologist has realized writing this process out has created positive brain waves, and he has become more detailed oriented. The other positive is negative thinking in task and multi-task are less because he is building a more specific oriented and more task-centered focus. Likewise, this psychologist says to keep it simple and create an environment of success rather than failure. If a fault occurs at his level in the detail-oriented task, then he reflects how he can learn from this?

This psychologist goal is three goals a day for six days a week. As God, he considers Sunday a day of rest and family day. This psychologist likes today and chill and reflect. The body and the mind need a day to disengage and have a relaxing and fun day. Three goals a day, six days in a week gives you a total of eighteen goals a week. The objective is to adjusted the days according and to make the negative days as limited as possible.

This author plans one day a week to use as the sweeping day. The day he uses is Sunday evening which he also uses for meditation and reflection. The sweep day is the day this author uses to complete task and goals through the week which were not completed or reflects on what caused the interruption. Reflection can occur on what could be different to make the goal complete for the given day. This psychologist uses this goal technique to underlines the reason a given target. For example, it could be procrastination or another goal became important. Sunday goal task for most of the time focuses on family tasks and home tasks. Sunday, as discussed above, should be time to set aside for family and friends and though this psychologist believes certain evenings can be set aside as well, the goal is always to increase the positive thinking and empowerment and at times just relaxing and decompressing is good for the mind and soul. The purpose of the three tasks goals is to refine one's priorities and to create a positive energy flow.

The objective in three tasked is to focus and create a feeling of accomplishment. The sense of accomplishment creates positive quantum brain waves. The goal task is also a way to master the day rather than let the day master the individual. A three-task goal system is a family-centered approach as well as God-focused. The focus for Sunday, as stated above, is to reflect on the gratitude and the love of family and share of God's love. The feeling of warmth and acceptance by the person's inner circle creates the positive waves in the brain and also positive empowerment because one is spending the time with close family and friends. The discussion above focuses on the calendar so let's get back to the debate.

The use of the calendar solidifies the free day for Sunday. The three-step system serves two objectives for the author. The first objective is the point of detail focus. For example, the author, in the past tended to focus not only a specific task but also would try to work on assignments for later in the week. Doing jobs which were not family focused created conflict in my past marriage because Sunday saw as a family day! Also, the focus becomes loss because the goal of the day is vague and not written down so this can create a "free will" mentality in the brain.

Secondly, the focus in any relationship or family, where children are involved, is spending time as a family. For example, many people will spend time in church or whatever religious ceremony of one's choosing. A substantial family gathering on Sunday increases the love among family members and higher positive energy. People often forget a support system is needed to accomplish challenging goals and tasks either at home or at work. One's support system relies on once a problematic day with the guidance and assistance to complete. A positive family-support system, who guides and directs the day can enhance the upcoming week. The tendency is lack family activity can lead to lower self-esteem and a feeling of failure for not completing the tasks, family time on Sunday, throughout the week. Ruling one's week, in essence, is creating ownership of the life a person wants to lead.

For example, writing the goals down, for this author, illustrates ownership in the day and the week. Property is critical in the empowerment in one's life. The goal is to remove all harmful neutrons and negative vibes. This author believes in writing the given task down also creates a foundation and commitment to completing the given goal or for the day. Once a target is complete there is always a feeling of a job well done or the feeling of accomplishment. Finishing a task or goal adds credibility to the day. For example, a person who finished a goal entirely and on time a sense of self-gratitude and increases self-esteem once a target is completed a small reward to oneself and a reflection of the good/bad in achieving the goal.

One of the three goals complete, the next step is to be reflective at the end of the day. Thoughtful and mediation can be five minutes to ten minutes a day. For this psychologist writing nightly in a journal creates this positive karma flow. The goal here is to be reflective but also find a personal niche which works for the individual. Remember this is all subjective and doing the right step, in one's mode, is critical for achieving more in life. The goal of the particular day is to show positive brain energy and growth. Find whatever method works for the person and wite in what form which works best for the person. For example, a person may use a computer; this author has a Google calendar but finds better results by writing the tasks down on paper. Here again, what works for one person may not work for another.

Additionally, this psychologist uses a daily reflective journal at night. The person must find when is the best time to write in a reflective mode. Some people tend to write better at night, while others tend to write very early in the morning. The goal for this psychologist, in his journal, is to set his mind within the correct framework. He manages to write his book around 11 pm till whatever the time he feels the energy has escaped him. He has written before 5 am. Further writing in creative mode enhances positive energy and exercises the brain.

Additionally, write when the spirit arises. This psychologist will force his brain to write by putting on spiritual music. There are days which he is not inspired to write, but this psychologist will write anyways to move the book projects further ahead. The goal is to write even if it is two pages or even a page. The goal is to at this attempt. Some times people will say they are too tired or will wait for tomorrow, but it both cases writing when one does not feel like it, which is some times, is still achieving some form of greatness. Reflection is part of understanding the person's strengths and weaknesses.

Understand one's weakness through this goal process can also enhance empowerment and growth. For example, reflection and mediation enhances understanding and accepting one's faults and turning the weaknesses into strengths. Additionally, re-reading part of this book will improve your areas of weakness. The author weaknesses in the past have focused on not being detail oriented and not breaking a commitment. For example, writing the reason one broke the promise can be ground-breaking and open new avenues to growth.

Writing and completing the task on paper forces the mind and rewires the brain. For example, this psychologist will write to improve his detailed oriented goals. Part of changing the weaknesses is focusing in on the behavior. Experience help shape behavior. The action is good or bad. This psychologist will often say a person is not good or bad but rather the person makes a poor choice in life. The goal is to change the unfortunate decision never to occur again.

The objective of any behavioral change focuses on creating a real task. Additionally, one must set a goal in changing the dangerous mission. The same is true for social work as well. Set a timeline to make the correct alignment and to follow through with reflection. Most scholars would say twenty-one to twenty-eight days is the time to change behavior. For example, in drafting this book, this psychologist sets a five-page limit a night and does not stop until the completion of the 5-pages per night. Once this complete he would like to draft additional books. He would like to complete at least three work of at least 130 pages each for the coming year. One of his goals in life, or should he say on his bucket list, has a top ten best seller book on the market. The goals are there amongst his professional goals, personal goals, and bucket list goals.

The objective is to have a 110-page book which can lead to the publisher by mid-May. The book is part of the process such as finishing his dissertation, finding a job in the therapy office, and spending time with family, and of course my BFF! Before completing my goal objectives, in the past, this psychologist let family and friends down, forgot dates, and cancel plans to do family activities such he can work on Sundays.

One has to have the right mental framework and to set a positive psychological approach to accomplish any given task. The objective is completing the work without delays. The accomplished goal is to mark ahead of time essential dates and family plans. One must set priorities and be proactive with one's time and day. The goal is not to let the day or week make a hostage of your plans. An empowered person controls their day and enables the energy to manage them. In other word let the universe play with one's day and make chaos and turmoil to the side. The goal is a focus on what the person knows her/his priorities are and where her/his goals need to be at any given time in space. One creates possibilities with the help of others and God! Keep open to change and the free to changing behavior to the positive side.

People tend to make goals at work but not out of the work environment. For example, in annual reviews, managers will discuss yearly goals achieved. The goals, in some cases, are hurried and not much thought about the goals. This psychologist worries about those professions who do ask for purposes at work. He also worries about manual labor jobs as well who do not ask employees about their intentions. The point here, most low-income people may have a lack of experience in creating goals, and this creates a problem. People all races and income need experience in working on their personal goals so their growth and empowerment can occur.

Many psychologist professionals discuss how to change behavior from a bad habit to a good pattern. This researcher has read many professionals on how to change practices. For example, authors such as Dr. Caroline Leaf say the process occurs within twenty-one days and have read authors such as Jim Rohn argue the behavior takes thirty days. This psychologist believes the focus should be on the person rather than the action. Many therapists analyze the act but not getting to the core of the individual. The individual is where the change has to occur and not on the hopes the person may change.

The core lies in what works for the client and not necessarily what works for this author or the therapist. Most therapists develop a road map, therapy, which can create growth and a change in the bad habit. In a lot of cases, this therapy will work for an individual, but this psychologist believes the ones who fail at changing the pattern may be the solution. The therapist should say in an ideal world what would you like to happen? Therapists and people put timelines on behavior patterns. Here again behavior patterns are subjective and should focus on a personal change for the individual.

The timeline to change the habit is subjective. Here again, this is all subjective upon the individual and is personable. The schedule can be for one person twenty-one days and another two months. Here it all depends on our wiring in our brain. Remember the objective is making a positive change and becoming more empowering in one's life. People try to make things more complicated by adding guidelines, charts, and stars. This psychologist believes in the old clique which, K.I.S.S. Keep it simple stupid. The goal kept it simple clear, doable and enjoyable to do the task at hand. Making goals feasible is the key to success.

When organizing one's day and planning the week, as discussed above, schedule the tasks as concise and straightforward as possible. The more specific the goal the chances of completing the goal is excellent. This psychologist recommends, changing a positive mindset the quickest and easiest way is to do the trivial things first and do the more significant things later. This psychologist thinks of ways of breaking down complex tasks. Doing the boring and mundane tasks first is an effective way to start the day. For example simple goals such as a combination of loading the dishwasher, putting the clothes in the dryer than in the closet, it is the best way to start a productive day. These are goals which written down maybe an excellent idea to start the day off right.

Some people chose to complete the most challenging task of the day. I agree, at times, this can be a necessity and may even be unavoidable, but for the most part, the focus should be doing the smallest task and moving forward and proactive in the day. When it comes to the more modest goals, one may say finish the job tomorrow. An argument may be it is easy to do and do the first thing in the morning. This psychologist analyzes goals on a scale one to three. One is the most important and three being the least important and then rating to see which should complete and in what order. He will do this and highlight goals which may cause problems later in the week. Highlighting helps this psychologist from targets, and events are not escaping the day. He further believes in finishing all tasks. He likes the old clique never put off tomorrow when you can finish today. The goal is to add the correct plans in one's life. This psychologist labels his list from important to less. The objective when planning the week is to see any areas where importance should address.

Further, on the thought of doing hard tasks at the beginning of the day, some people are completing the most hardened task at the beginning of the day which may bring relief but if the day is a third-way completed one may not have the energy or the willpower to achieve the two-thirds of the day. This psychologist believes in pacing oneself through the day. Be realistic in one's approach through the day. Be realistic in what one can accomplish within a given day. The three-task system can be flexible if one is having a busy week. For those who are doing must-jobs or have full-time status at home and working this psychologist recommends trying a two-tank system. Remember the whole thing here is subjective and do what works best for the individual.

For example, if one is a single mom, works a ten-hour day, the solution may be to work on two tasks for the day, as stated above, so the person does not feel overwhelmed and hopeless. Here again, this psychologist is not saying two tasks system may be ideal when things are a bit hectic in life. This psychologist experience depicts how three task day in the modern, hectic world is the correct number to accomplish your tasks for that given day.

Here again, it is subjective. This psychologist likes to read other "help books" who say their method works and the best way to break a habit is repetition. Sometimes the duplication by the person can create hostility and bad vibes. The best approach in any new technique and learning is to try new ways of learning and figuring the best strategy for the person to receive maximum results. The book is a set of guidelines (foundation) to work your mindset to transform into a positive and healthy outcome.

Here again, this psychologist, for example, will use Sunday afternoon to plan his schedule for the week. He takes time late afternoon and writes down on a piece of paper things he believes are essential to complete during the week. Planning cannot occur in fifteen minutes. Writing requires at least an hour in reflection and writing things down.

The point is to plan one's week consider. For the author, this exercise in preparing the week, fine tunes his detail-oriented skills. The goal of any mental activity is to strengthen one's mind and create positive spiritual energy. The author plays music classical music, new age, or a bit of rock and roll now and then. The goal of this exercise is to stimulate his writing ability. One must know what works best (niche) to complete this writing exercise. For example, one week it could be Vivaldi and the "Four Seasons" or the next week it may be the Beatles "Rubber Soul" or even Johnny Cash. It depends on what can be the most productive in the time frame.

Additionally, the phone is off or put on Airplane Mode, so no distractions can occur to accomplish the given task. This author reads authors such as Tony Robbins and Tommy Baker who say reward oneself once the work completed. My problem is when this psychologist is writing he can distract. The goal for him is to pay himself once complete a writing task. For this author, the author will compose for 50 minutes and then take a fifteen-minute break.

For additionally task, such as completing this book, the author writes for an hour, has a page limited he plans to accomplish in a day and then rewards himself. Further, since most writing is subjective and in one's perspective, completing one's tasks one must figure the best time for writing. I use the task time for Sunday afternoons, but since some of my best books occurs at night (a night owl), I write the time which is more favorable for the task. As stated above, pick the best time for oneself and complete the daily work for the week.

This psychologist views thing in his perspective. In other words, complete writing is the best opportunity time for the wring to be productive. As stated above, this psychologist writes at night when it is less hectic, and he feels the best energy in his writing. This author knows of friends who will write in the morning when the person feels most productive. The point is to find a place where to limit distractions and maximize one's writing and in self-reflective mode.

This psychologist argues a word of caution if for some reason an emergency occurs, and one knows the writing will not happen on Sunday the weekly planner will assist one in making the best day to accomplish the task. For example, if the author has a busy week and knows there is a family commitment for Sunday the weekly plan may be to use Saturday as the alternate day. The goal here is NOT to let this fall into the beginning of the work week because the chances are one will lose the momentum. When this author was in graduate school, the first thing he learned is always to know papers, research, and commitment in school and the work occurred on the weekends. The objective is to take account a complete task which acts in proactively. One must consider those days and plan, plan plan. Planning is a strength of this author, and his objective is to keep things orderly ad not to caught forgetting key dates. Ignoring critical times is rarely occurs to him but those days which the tasks miss or forgotten adjustments.

For example, researchers illustrate the more one focus on given task the likelihood the person feels she/he can empower the day. Focusing on three tasks or less in a given day adds happiness and the sense of work completed right. Doing multi-task during the day can be overwhelming and lead to disappear and hopelessness.

Writing down six or seven goals within a given day chance are most people will not accomplish the list for the day. For example, a person completes, it's a good day, and the karma is flowing and maxing, the person can achieve four goals for the day. One task to finish tomorrow and the day is Monday. This author depicts how in the beginning people can control the series of functions. It is when the day gets complicated, and the adjustments need to occur to keep one's sanity through the process of the day.

The person then has one goal for Tuesday. Their day hijacked and was not able to complete, and objectives for Tuesday but luckily Wednesday is "hump day," and the person feels they can complete the four tasks without any problems. Wednesday the person achieved two goals. Two goals into Thursday. Three goals from Thursday now have five goals to bring to completion. Thursday the person can finish two tasks. Three works from Thursday and three from Friday. A total of six functions for Friday.

Well, it's Friday, the end of the week, and the person because the end of the week completes two tasks. Four tasks are going into Saturday.

Plus, the three functions for Saturday gives the person seven tasks. Two of the job focus on work-related projects so these two tasks will carry into Monday so instead of having three tasks for Monday, now the person has five. The five tasks illustrate the problem people get behind in the week and never catch up to the weekly assignments. The result produces a complicating and negative week. The result is people lose focus. Once focus is loss dilemma and stress set in. The objective is to keep the list concise and to the point. The point here illustrates if a person focusses or an emergency occurs such as a death in the family, the focus is a loss. The key is reflective and is honest in one's ability to achieve their perspective goals.

Once the person begins to write their tasks for the first week, adjustments will have to occur. The person needs to focus on the functions and see how the week and the feature work in one's favor. The objective to create better empowerment and change in one's life. The goals for a shift in empowerment focus on one's commitment to accomplish the plans for a given week. The process is doing the exact steps in changing a mindset to a positive framework. Secondly, people tend to distract throughout the day and with the aid of social media, televisions, and cell phones people seem to lose focus of the assigned tasks. This author sees this more in the GEN Millennials and children born after 2000.

They're interaction with bot GEN groups, and the lack of social interaction has hampered the distraction of these generations. The point here for both generations time away from the cell phone, especially on the weekends, may increase focus. This psychologist knows this hurts production in the workforce by observing people pick up the phone when the phone should be in a desk drawer or airplane mode. Companies are now implementing no cell phones in the work environment, and this psychologist sees this happening more on a grander scale. For example, has anyone ever been in church or at a ceremony when one has heard a cell phone go off? Interruptions with cell phones on can be disturbing to the service, and as stated above, more organization will eventually create harsh cell phone policies. The point this psychologist makes one must be aware of their weakness and if the fault is abuse to cell phone use action by the individual needs to be addressed to regain focus.

This new focus will create positive energy within the brain (quantum) which will allow for better critical thinking and agendas. The goal in any written or essential tasks of thought is to engage both hemispheres of the brain. A person who both regions are active can enhance their productivity and their empowerment in life. For example, this psychologist develops my tasks on my desk which can be readily available. The point here this psychologist tends to be more visual and vocal in remembering things. The goal here is to understand if a person is oral or visual. One has to follow their learning capability.

This psychologist uses a voice recorder as well, but since his strengths are visual, he will use more visual aids. For example, he uses a small pile of 3X5 blank cards on his desk to write things down. The purpose is for his strength as a visual person writing and seeing the writing increases the memory in his brain. The aim here is to activate not only the conscious mind but the sub-conscious mind as well.

The goal of the 3X 5 index cards is the sub-conscious will at times bring things forward to the conscious ideas or feelings which should write down on in some form. The mind is a very expansive and complex organ. Thoughts, concepts, and interaction occur throughout the day with people, ideas, and whatever the brain figures can be a threat and or pleasure to the body. Having index cards near one's desk or within a short walking distance after bedtime can help format a solid next day. The thing is to write the thought down on a card and re-visit the view the following morning. This author has sent emails to my BFF, in the middle of the night, to clarify things he felt she did not understand or how he thought about a specific situation. The writing on the index cards when a thought occurs solidifies the goals and objectives for the week. This psychologist has learned creating positive energy is the key to success in a happy and healthy lifestyle. Part of this process is placing the brain in a proactive mode rather than a reactive mode. Part of this process is the right tasks, and goals in sequences create less stress and anxiety for the mind as well as the body.

This author has found when he plans something during the week, some ideal or event eventually falls through and forgets. Therefore, this author; will write things he needs to accomplish in one card and other card things which he wants to achieve during the coming week. This author sees a difference between what a person needs to complete and what a person needs to succeed.

This psychologist sees it is there is a difference between a need and a wasn't. This author examines more in what than in demand. The value in wanting is to accomplish a task rather than needing to perform a function. Want for this author, in the same thing as shoulds and musts, is something that is a high priority and this task has a completion date. For example, this author needs to write five pages a day for the next twenty-one days to complete this book. He wants to write five pages a day for twenty-one days because the author sees more weight in the word want than in need. He knows he needs to go to the grocery store sometime today and by cleaning supplies, but this is a task if required, can complete tomorrow as well.

Though this may be somatic in word choice, it is all about what works for the individual. See I even used the word want in the last sentence. The goal here is to do what works for the individual. This psychologist is keen to people use of vocabulary and the proper message a person is trying to be about in their conversation. The goal of his interaction with people is finding the correct usage and the right way to bring about a positive approach to the message. This psychologist will confirm in conversations is this a need or is this a want. Develop their niche in critical thinking and finding the karma which works for them is the essential thing in a person. The goal as this author has started to see what works best for the individual in any given situation and always remember nothing set in stone other than what you want to change and transform in your mindset. Remember the goal is to convert one's mindset from a negative perspective to a positive attitude.

Finally, when it comes to the weekly planning, nothing is set into stone and the emphasis on being open to changes within the week. The main focus is to concentrate on the given week and not to look too forward. This psychologist likes to live in the "present" and thinks the best solution is to keep one eye on the week but to focus on the given day. One may get an urgent call Monday night, and the three tasks may have to adjust for Tuesday. Here again, the objective is not the day to controls one life, but for the person to seize the day. The clique which says you take on the day is the focus of creating a positive mental outlook.

The second step in the three-step process is acting. The action is moving the ideal or task forward. People have had plans to do things or achieve goals in their life, but the person lacks the alternate approach. For example, drug additions can be a bit of a problem for many people. This psychologist classifies drugs as any substance that is foreign to the body. Alcohol is just one to mention. For example, this author sees alcohol as a drug because it can inhibit cognitive and sound thinking. For example, this psychologist does not drink because he sees this behavior, drinking, can affect his A game and this psychologist believes he always must have his best approach forward in any given situation. This psychologist did drink in the past, but the next day he would feel that something is not right, and he felt this took a step back from his best A game. Athletics sports, state at times, the playing field is a game of inches. Inches is the same in life as well. If this author feels the intake of a substance will cause him me to think slower wake slower and not be as enthusiastic, that is why to do something which can affect one's day which may harm the brain or body should take into consideration.

Here again, this is subjective, this psychologist knows people who drink, and it does not have any effect on their day, but alcohol has an impact on this psychologist day which is harmful, and this psychologist likes a positive influence throughout the day. Example, this author can bring his A game on less sleep, and this can be destructive for others. My daughter and BFF, on the other hand, needs her eight hours of sleep or they cannot function through the day. Here again one must find their groove in life and the karma (bad or good) which works for them. Stretching the personal growth and seeing the pattern which works is the key to success.

One must be willing when acting their day, be prepared to accept one's wins and your defeats — ideal and strategies which works and fails in positive mental growth. People are eager to try something new until the failure sets in and the individual gives up. This psychologist has this experience occasionally and knows one has always had to keep a positive mindset and create the possibility.

Here this author will occasionally review Napoleon Hill book, "Think and Grow Rich." The book though written many years ago works on the mental concept on how to think and grow rich. This author also sees this as how to think set a series of thoughts in one's mind to be positive. Each time this psychologist picks this book up, he reads, and he learns something new. The goal in action is to gain critical concepts or strategies to make a person stronger in a weaker area in the mind and body. This process in action calls a win.

Wins increase your will power to overcome obstacles. This psychologist sees the value in the big wins as well as the small successes. Researchers depict the small triumphs added up over time can create the big wins. Setting goals and objectives and add up to wins. In each case, award systems should set in place on small and significant gains. As this author is typing, this late at night, he has a goal of writing five pages a day. This goal is almost accomplished, and he plans to listen to some Al Green, The Preacher, to mellow his day. In rewarding on the big wins celebrate by doing something big. Depending on the significant gains once the Ph.D. complete a trip to the beach will is a plan with my family. For example, when this psychologist completed his M.A., he took his friends and family out to dinner! Celebrate those bug victories with those you love because this adds to one's empowerment and growth in life.

Losses should be a reflective time, and one should not get down on themselves. Injuries should be opportunities and learning experiences. This author dated a person in my early twenties, and we broke up. This author feels into a very deep Depression and understands how people can get so low. This feeling was "Hellish," and there were days this author could not get out of bed. I do remember a conversation with my mother telling me to pull it all together or her and my dad were going to put me in a mental hospital. Though I do not fault my parents for their lack of concern, this author for some reason, was able to work himself out of this "Hellish" state and move his life forward. To this day, this author did not know what day or when it happened but something clicked and just like the most profound and darkest night the sun rises, and a new day begins. The other as the tide goes out the wave will eventually return. All this is mental action and creates a positive emotion within the brain.

Losses should reflect what can one learn from this situation. Instead of a passive-aggressive behavior look at the case and see what one can learn and try not to make the same mistakes. Losses should be a growth opportunity and to make the BEST of the situation and turn that favorable situation into a proactive. For example, instead of lacking a car the objective is how to get around without the help of a vehicle. The

The goal is to take some form of action rather than wait for the right time to make the plan. I learned to go to Arizona for research; there is never an appropriate time. The best thing is to make the plan and stick with the project. As stated above, even the best-made plans never go the way the program should go but if one is in the right framework rather than the negative approach success is sure to come. For this psychologist, fear is the unknown, and the risk of the unknown can be a bit overwhelming for him. The goal is to take the first step. Steve Harvey has a video "everybody has to Jump" I find this an excellent reflective tool to learn when one jumps terrible things will happen, but at some point, one will begin to fly. As Steve Harvey says, You Got to Jump!

Acting can lead to remarkable success but as stated above the goal is to transform one's life for the better. Acting means taking personal responsibility for one's actions. This psychologist argues with the rise of entitlements, by individuals, who can be in the workforce, people feel and except for the government to supply their basic needs. This psychologist agrees people disabled, elderly, or in early childhood development given the entitlements because of the immediate need to support people who lack the means to help themselves. Today, the objective to improve one's life, the process starts by becoming more empowered in believing the individual can and will better their lives. - If as a society, we are enabling more to the poor and the lower class, this psychologist believes with the correct teaching more impoverished communities can live a better life for themselves and can impact others within their communities.

The emphasis in the past, especially in the bigger cities, is to improve the lives of people for example, in the city of Cincinnati, Ohio. Spending money in the town seems to focus on one to three areas within a given community, which is umbrellaed under the city. Years ago, in the mid-twenty-century, community development was the center in the focus of growth. For example, in Cincinnati, the West End or Over the Rhine is where increase occurred until blight occurred within these communities. The people were involved in the community, and the money stayed in these communities. Once blight form there seems to be a disconnect by most of the people with the city.

The rise of suburbia in the late twenty-century, a disengagement occurred, and many cities lost the revenue of the people within these communities. Central cities led to higher crime and higher unemployment in these communities. Loss of good jobs led to people needing assistance, entitlements, from the federal government. The example of the West End, in Cincinnati Ohio is an example of this process.

This psychologist believes this effort of looking at the city as a whole (micro) should go to improving the lives of the people with a given community. The goal should shift back to the approach of local communities. Focusing on the cities, which to be honest is happening to specific neighborhoods, West End can create empowerment and ownership by the local people within the communities.

Empowering individuals with the local communities would create well-being and a sense of belonging which will lead to provide for the community and lower crime in the community. For example, if individual life in city A and he/she feels a belonging within the district, if a drug house should appear, the residence will take issue with the home with the drug house.

The "Baby Boomers" felt the need to move and dwell out in the suburbs while communities failed. Upward mobility creates a loss of ownership and respect; hence the crime rate increases within these local communities, not all but quite a few developed blight and decay. Cities would stay proactive would have people interested in their communities and less disease. Thomas Moore talked of this type of Utopia in his book but the foundation of ownership respect and love for all can exist with proper city planning, and the politics realign.

All government lands should return to the proper ownership of the native people. This psychologist also believes all Native Tribe Lands turn to the local tribes and not be in the care of the federal government. Tribal lands would create a sense of belonging, after many years of moved off native lands and create opportunities to focus on the growth of the cities and the poor rural towns. All national forest and national parkland as well should turn over to the local states or communities who know the best interests of those lands as well. The concern by the government should be a careful eye in these lands misappropriated or misused for the wealth of the few. Miss use coincides with the native lands as well. This author firmly believes native tribes such as the Sioux (Black Hills) have the authority of these lands and the government should require their sovereign rights to the native tribes. This author believes letting the tribes dictate their sovereign rights will create better harmony in the reservations. Empowering and loving local communities develop a bond of friendship and respect for all those in the given population.

Granted and this author firmly believes this will not occur overnight, but at least the step would increase additional funding for the federal government where the money used in more likely areas such as education and welfare. The point is as a society we need to act to create positive minds and influences less dependency on drugs.

Once empowering emerges, the next tool for allowing is teaching. Many of these communities have centers but lack the funding and the commitment from people within the community. Instructing people, the value and respect in the given community can create programs for the elderly (more engaged and enhanced) and application such as Early Child Development. As stated above, this is a community focused in major and rural cities. For example, Benson Arizona, after the Great Recession, is still trying to recoup their losses from the departure of loss business. Benson is a rural community about 40 miles East of Tucson Arizona. Crating funding and involving the residence within a community can increase the impact of growth in the city. Depending less on Social Services which is a mandate by specific federal regulations may improve more well-being amongst the local people in the town.

The loss of focus in many of these rural cities has been an increase in unemployment or people living outside and not working within the community. With less revenue in these small rural towns, local benefits are less, and people go without services needed. Here again, the loss focus and lower income may create a generation of low education and people who require to be on government entitlements. What is occurring it the lack of action by the federal state level and the movement needs to happen with the specific county or community. If training centers exist in these areas, people can learn a skill and train. The goal is to create action and empowerment by getting people off government assistance and be better empowerment for the families within a specific community.

This psychologist envisions an increase in industries automation within the next twenty years, and the need for unskilled labor will demise. Communities such as Benson Arizona will have an existence of future blight and future where people will have to depend on the government for assistance. The concern for this psychologist people must learn a skilled trade so the people can have self-worth and provide for their family. Here again, the emphasis is on the action by the community to create great empowerment for the individual and the communities. If people feel empowered and feel they have a decent income to support their family, those people and communities will flourish. In other words, as stated above, those communities who invest in the people within the community by action such as daycare, childhood development, and training centers will stand to survive within the middle twenty-first century. Those communities who do not act will continue to see the rise of blight and the departure of people who can make a difference within the given society. Losing people who can enhance action within a community can have an impact on the town.

The objective is not the government responsibility to take care of the individual, but the community in which the individual resides. Maslow needs chart illustrates at the top a sense of self-worth and belonging. Cities who become proactive rather than keeping the status quo will have a better chance to survive than those who stay passive and except the government to aid them. An example would be communities who actively search out the people within the given population to be proactive and shape the city. The focus would be on the people and less on the reliability of Social Services. With much waste on Social Services, the direction seems to comply with state and federal regulations rather than the wants within the local communities. Here again, the focus is community development and belong not state. Growth is an action which creates a positive mindset for the individuals within the local communities.

Empowering others within a community is instructing people in the given population. For instance, going back and reviewing Cincinnati Ohio. Many cities have lower elementary schools programs within their communities. These schools are community-based for parents who do not have to travel distances to take their children to school. The community school which existed in the mid-twenty centuries was community focused since transportation limit, and sense belongs existed in towns such as Hartwell. Since Hartwell is part of Cincinnati, many teachers do not live in the city so the focus on community. This psychologist believes education should be at the local level and not be the responsibility of the government nor the state.

Funding belongs to the people within a specific community and like in the past if the city has an excellent school system people will stay within the community. Having pride in the community enhances ownership and belonging within the community. For example, for the Cincinnati School District, the focus is on the city as a whole and not on the given towns. Granted this may be at the elementary level as a sense of belonging but this psychologist sees the value in local school should be K-12 grades. Here again, the school district should be analyzing if the school segregate or misappropriation of funds is occurring. Communities schools should be available for anyone whether race, creed or sexual orientation. The problem arises with private schools, such as Catholic schools, causes the demand for an excellent education. The psychologist believes if the local community school is viable and top-notch people will attend the school rather than pay the expenses of a private school.

The belief exists in many suburbia schools, especially in larger cities, local school districts hide their inferior teaching ability to teach children which leads them to pass children grade after grade. In essence, suburbia sees the inner cities schools as inferior. Inner-city schools, on the contrary, is lack of support by suburbia. If the local schools become parent-focused, parents would have to INVEST in their local school rather than bus or commute outside the private city schools. To aid in the advancement of public education, those wishing to attend a private school would pay an additional tax to support the local school. Community schools will lower the admission to individual private schools since many of these primary and secondary school cost as much as the first year in college. Some would argue as a psychologist is this fair to tax a person attending a school outside their community? The answer is yes because the resources and the revenue the individual is paying can is within the specific city. The objective here is to create a sense of belonging and action with the school system, within the community and since the person is attending a school outside the district a gap (ownership) exist.

Further, community schools which prosper are those who offer the best education at the public level.

The third step in the three-step process is reflective. The key in any change for behavior in life is to reflect if the difference has an impact on one's life. The point here is to see the effect of the action is a positive or negative effect. Positive responses can be a reflective thought process by is the behavior added or helping one change their life. An example could be weight loss and how this can have an impact on someone who is having a health issue. The point here is in every aspect of one's life being reflective and analyzing how I can make changes in one's life creates higher empowerment and transformation.

This psychologist is analyzing the good and the bad in all aspects of his life and always questioning whether he can do more to improve his experience. This author sees his confident demeanor and how his positive outlook in life has an impact on others in his life. The first step in his analyzing is how this behavior impacts others around him.

Analyzing how the behavior impacts others around him is a beautiful way to know how to make changes in the described action. One of my activities in life is to engage others in discussions. This psychologist finds certain people he would not have a conversation because of the lack of personable connection. What this psychologist means is how this person energy level is a positive to home or s this person has a negative energy level. This psychologist has a challenging time helping those with a shallow negative energy level and does he best to help those with this level become he is uncomfortable with their negativity and tries to change their outlook on life.

The point here this psychologist sees his life as trying to help others, but as life always goes, once we are out of the comfort zone, we become a bit confused due to areas of uncertainty in life. This psychologist is open-minded and is always open to the possibilities in life but when he examines areas he accomplishes so he becomes a bit anxious in life. For example, on his third residency for school, he was a bit talkative and a bit overconfident in things he did over the weekend. The exercise where he had to do power point presentation was a bit rushed at the time, and he did complete the task. Upon future observation, the director was upset that this person rushed the project and a few words misspelled words in the PowerPoint. The reflection here was a bit humbling and realized that this psychologist must be careful about any of his projects.

At first, this was troubling to me and created a negative outlook. Upon deeper reflection and letting things settle for a few days this psychologist realized the importance of what this experience could teach me. Upon future review and thought-provoking time, this psychologist learns when viewing a situation, the outcome is what is this experience teaching me currently. This framework, reflection, on what this situation or experience is what this psychologist says to himself. The point here does not view it as a negative but what can this experience teach me at the time.

James Redfield authored a book which focuses on psychological and spiritual ideas rooted in Eastern thought and New Age Spirituality. One point this book and my book would like to connect is meaningful coincidences where consciousnesses will accelerate. Meaningful coincidences people can explain this are noticing in their lives. If a person has negative thoughts or blockage due to stress or the inability to communicate with others information loss. James Redfield believes:

Relating to others. This insight comes in several pieces.

- Children raise without control dramas if they have constant, undivided access to an adult who can give them the energy they need.
- Development block by an "addiction to another person." The subtle energy has a male and female side. If you can access one and someone else the other, then for a brief time the couple can fill with energy. But the focus on the other person eventually cuts each off from the universal energy. The two begin competing for power, restarting control dramas. This is the falling-in-love/falling-out-of-love phenomenon.
- Everyone who crosses our path has a message for us. We should give them energy and help them get clear so that we can accurately deliver the message.
- Other people's control dramas will break down if we name them and refuse to play a role in them.

In each of the illustration above, especially the second one has a male and female side. One does not have to be female to have feminine energy, and this holds for males. The premise here is one must know their energy level and the breaking point in the energy flow. The question of how the person knows their flow depends

Spirit Article discusses the difference between the classification. The brain separates into two hemispheres. The left hemisphere seen as practical, logical, and focused to the point. It likes to follow the rules;

it sees things as black and white and is more like a computer program that sees data and makes a judgment on the data — the left-brain views by many scholars as to the male-dominated part of the brain.

The right brain sees being more creative, it flows all over the place with ideas and suggestions, it takes it time and does not follow the rules, and it is free-spirited in its direction. Between both spheres of the brain the person develops situations, good or bad, and balance logic and creativity. As discussed in the Spirit article on emotional health/mental health this psychologist belief, is people have both elements within them, yet the person often leans more towards one side depending on our conditioning, personality, environment, and social settings. Both teams are equally important to balance, and when a person has too much of one kind of energy, the person can begin to shut down and reject the opposing power as being 'wrong' as opposed to seeing the benefits of it

The key here we must manage this energy and reflect on what side of the brain we are most robust and work on the weak side so that we can have a balance sphere. My objective as a psychologist has a balanced mind and not one stronger than the other. This psychologist believes that just like the body one must exercise the brain. All one needs to do is Google, and one can create exercises for the mind. Though I do not practice this every day. I do have programs that enhance brain growth.

The keys are to be reflective in one's approach to changing the negative thought pattern to a definite thought pattern. This psychologist practices this every day. One other tool to use in this approach of being reflective is writing in a daily journal. This psychologist discussed this above, the point in writing in a journal enhances the reason why someone is in the state of negativity. Analyzing one's mental ups and down can be a clue in those good and bad days. This psychologist believes that food allergies can have an impact on our thinking process. The key is to pinpoint the days where one feels they are not on their A game.

I discussed this briefly at the top about being on one's A game. This psychologist believes one cannot be on their A game every day of the week, but one can be close as they can be concerned about being at their best performance. Granted, even this psychologist has its ebb and flows, one he calls the great karma days and the bad karma days. It is all reflective of what one views as critical in their daily life. For me finishing a Ph.D. in psychology has been a long and tedious task. The goal of this psychologist is a sense of events and actions moving forward continuously.

The daily writing enhances this by examining whether he is on his A game for the week or has there been an issue as to why things are not going the way he envisions. For instance, this author has a problem with occurring sinus affections and at times will slow his thought process down. He also sees the impact of the sinus infections which occur because his immune system is weak, because of the lack of sleep or some food group he eats such as gluten. The goal is always in his mind, is to watch the intake of certain food groups which can have an impact on his critical thinking skills.

Another product this psychologist concern is his diet in soft drinks. The nutrition value is minimal, and the impact that sugar has on his life is critical as well. He learned that the more soda one's drinks the likelihood mental fatigue will step in as well as a sugar crash from taking in high fructose corn syrup. Granted, to have this product occasionally is a great suggestion. People often say well drink the diet sodas but to be honest, this psychologist believes the diet sodas are worse than the regular sodas. All mixers have caffeine which is not suitable for the brain as well.

Caffeine improves people in performance in a range of tasks such as response time and information processing. Caffeine shows some improvement in proofreading tasks, but the research is scarce. Most people drink coffee, tea, or soda which contain copious amounts of caffeine. Verywellmind illustrates that comparisons between those who take a low dosage of caffeine (100 mg caffeine per day) and those who consume a lot more (300mg per day) that the improvements are quite small and do not get better with larger dosages of caffeine.

The point here is the reaction to counteracting the caffeine can be the effects of caffeine addiction. So, the person is getting closer to their performance because of the caffeine addiction. If one is to remove the habit slowly, the production may in fact increase. This psychologist sees like any chemical can inhibit the growth of the brain and neutrons.

Further, the enhanced intake of caffeine will not increase performance. The short-term benefit from caffeine is anxiety or depression. The other downside of a large intake of caffeine is withdrawal symptoms which will impair one's mental process. A better strategy is lower the dosage of caffeine to one or two cups a day and time the caffeine intake to getting the best effects without the withdrawal which will require one's full attention.

This author loves to drink green tea. His consumption limited to the evening hours, or he will have difficulty sleeping at nights. His goal recently as argued above is limit his intake to the morning hours and drink water or pineapple juice and conduct water in the late afternoon or evenings. Tea has enabled him to be more productive during the day and is allowing him to sleep better at nights. Writing in the journal made him aware of his shortcomings. The point here when writing the memoir, he is reflective of where gaps in learning or where he did not feel his best. The position as stated above is thoughtful and to learn what works best for an individual.

The other point here to make is the use of other drugs to enhance the feeling of euphoria or to dull the senses of pain. The point with any improved medication is that it can influence the performance outcome of the individual. The best advice is any substance which can inhibit one's growth is not highly recommend putting into the money. This psychologist sees the value in those terminally ill or in need of numbing drugs to lower the pain. The point here for the person who wants to improve their life, wanting to be one's best every day can accomplish if a person respects their mind. Drugs in any form can enhance performance in the short-term, but the concern should be in the long-term effects on the brain and mental growth. In the National Institute on Drug Abuse for Teachers

The use of vitamins and others stimulates to aid the health of the body is an acceptance for the mind and the spirit. This psychologist believes, like anything else, over stimulus usage can have an impact on the body and mind. In my observations of men and women who use steroids or other drugs which increase muscle. For example, anabolic steroids may trigger aggression behavior in some people. Those who abuse anabolic steroids may have a behavior shift in which the media terms "roid rages." When the steroid user stops using the drug depression along with suicidal tendencies can occur. The other concern here is the effects it has on family relationships and routing behavior in mind.

The hypothalamus controls one's testosterone level within the body. This function within the brain controls appetite, blood pressure, moods, and creative ability. Like any drug that enters the body, it breaks down and enters the bloodstream. Drugs enter the bloodstream, then the drug transported throughout the whole body. In this case, the anabolic steroids change the message to the hypothalamus. Medications in many forms disrupt normal hormone function. For men, anabolic steroids interfere with the average production of testosterone and cause the testes to shrink. And low sperm count. In women, anabolic steroids may cause a loss of monthly periods by signaling to the hypothalamus and the reproductive organs, growth of body, and deepening of the voice. One thing that concerns this psychologist is when people who do these shows and the weight training the effect it has on them in middle age and the amount of Depression or Anxiety these people will feel.

My point here is not to take away from peoples improving their looks by enhancing drugs, but this is a multi-million-dollar business, and the concern here is how much protection does the average consumer know or is aware of these altering drugs. This author believes we should get back to the basic of eating more salads, lowering our intake and picking the right food groups to consume. This author thinks this is part of the reflection in life as well.

The other concern is the reproduction for women and the effect this has on their child-bearing years. This psychologist believes the truth be known a lot of unknowns exist for some of these drugs and since fitness and health are the fabs of the first twenty-first center he wonders if the pendulum has begun to swing the other way. This author believes people must be reflective and educated in the drugs they intake into their bodies. This researcher believes in the principle at what cost are we willing to pay to have a lean and muscular body and does this facade tell a person who they are. Looks are subjective as the mind is subjective but if we change the shape to the image God did not want the person to be is that be subjective? Food for thought.

Though this book is not on people's behavior, this psychologist observes people who will post have half-clothed photos of them on Instagram or Facebook centering on their weight loss or how they have conquered gaining strength or flattening their abdomen. The critical point here is to be cognitive of their environment and what the person is trying to achieve in the process. This author feels people need respect and understanding but showing very sexy body parts may not be sending the right message to people. Here again, as stated above this psychologist believes people look for acceptance and acknowledgment rather than the consequences of a flaw action. The author is not here to criticize a person but for growth to occur this psychologist believes sound judgments need to happen in life. Judging people is not the case here; it is reflective of behavior.

This psychologist sees this as acceptance of an individual not as a mental thriving human being but as a piece of candy. In this age of "Me Too" as a society are we not comprising are values when we see people on not who they are but are of something else. The goal in life is to be genuine, sincere, and present and this psychologist is to blame as well for looking at this and making not a rude comment but a comment that this person is beautiful. This psychologist is being reflective and sees the value in one end in social media, to grow one's psychology practice, but the other purpose where social media can be disruptive and harmful in his view of people. The point he draws on is good may out weight the bad but still the bad here is not he sees as social norms.

Here are twenty-five empowerments by recognized leaders in the field of leadership. Empowering one's employees is a top priority but also important is the person allowing themselves and take full accountability of their action. Empowerment is real in many professions as well such as education and social workers. The following comes from an article on Linkedin in empowering employees. *If Empowering Your Employees isn't a Top Priority, It Should Be* The completed list includes twenty-five. This psychologist recommends ten on the list and to say the ten affirmations daily for thirty days. Please chose t the ones who can have the most significant impact on empowering one's life.

1. *"My job as a leader is to make sure that everybody in the company has great opportunities and they feel they are having a meaningful impact on the good of society." — Larry Page, Google*

2. *"It's not the tools you have faith in. Tools are just tools — they work, or they don't work. It's the people you have faith in or not. —Steve Jobs*

3. *"In technology, it's about the people: getting the best people, retaining them, nurturing a creative environment and helping to find a way to innovate." —Marissa Mayer, Yahoo*

4. *"You know how, as most entrepreneurs do, that a company is only as good its people. The hard part is building the team that will embody your company culture and propels you forward." — Kathryn Minshew, The Muse*

5. *"To be the best place to buy you must be the best place to work. Treat your employees the way you want your customers to be treated, maybe even better." —Shep Hyken, customer service expert*

6. *"The organization is, above all, social. It is people." —Peter Drucker*

7. *"Businesses often forget about the culture and ultimately they suffer for it, because they cannot deliver good service from unhappy employees." —Tony Hsieh, Zappos*

8. *"Start with why customers will never love a company until the employees love it first." —Simon Sinek*

9. *"People want guidance, not rhetoric; they need to know what the plan of action is and how it will implement. They want to be given responsibility to help solve the problem and the authority to act on it." —Howard Schultz, Starbucks*

10. *"No company, small or large, can win over the long run without energized employees who believe in the mission and understand how to achieve it." —Jack Welch, General Electric*

11. *"We believe that if you get the culture right, most of the other stuff, like great customer service, or building a great long-term brand or*

empowering passionate employees and customers, will happen on its own." —Tony Hsieh, Zappos

12. *"First get the right people on the bus, the wrong people off the bus, and the right people in the right seats, and then they can figure out where to drive it." —Jim Collins, Good to Great*

13. *"Hire for attitude and train for skills." — Tom Peters*

14. *"If each of us hires people who are smaller than we are, we shall become a company of dwarves, but if each of us hires people who are bigger than we are, we shall become a company of giants." — David Ogilvy*

15. *"Human beings are not things needing to be motivated and controlled. They are four-dimensional: body, mind, heart, and spirit." —Stephen Covey*

16. *"We believe that when the right talent meets the right opportunity in a company with the right philosophy, amazing transformation can happen." —Reid Hoffman*

17. *"You cannot have faith in people unless you take action to improve and develop them." —Sumantra Ghoshal*

18. *"The inventory, the value of your company, walks out the door every evening." —Bill Gates*

19. *"The task of leadership is not to put passion into people, but to inspire and elicit it — for the passion is there already." —Ty Howard*

20. *"You don't build a business, you build people, then people build the business." —Zig Ziglar*

21. *"The best executive is the one who has sense enough to pick good men to do what he wants to be done, and self-restraint enough to keep from meddling with them while they do it." —Theodore Roosevelt*

22. *"Virtually every company will be going out and empowering their workers with a certain set of tools, and the big difference in how much value is received from that will be how much the company steps back and really thinks through their business processes, thinking through how their business can change, how their project*

management, their customer feedback, their planning cycles can be quite different than they ever were before." —Bill Gates

23. *"Power can be taken, but not given. The process of the taking is empowerment in itself."* —Gloria Steinem

24. *"Never tell people how to do things. Tell them what to do, and they will surprise you with their ingenuity."* —General George S. Patton.

25. *"An empowered organization is one in which individuals have the knowledge, skill, desire, and opportunity to personally succeed in a way that leads to collective organizational success."* —Stephen Covey

Conclusion

The above discussion focuses on empowerment and a change which can occur if a person develops the right framework for reform. Though the process is subjective to the individual difference and empowerment can arise if the person additionally puts into motion the correct mindset to change. The problem arises with people when the feeling of hopelessness and anxiety occurs, and the person has no avenues to turn but tries to exist day to day. People will use the lottery to gain wealth, but this is a flaw in reasoning because instant wealth does not ensure happiness. The only way to accomplish a healthy and happy lifestyle is being empowered in a person's life and be willing to accept responsibility in life.

Endnotes

http://ww3.capsim.com/modules/downloads/ethics/pdf/Strategies_for_Ethical_Reasoning.pdf

http://www.drjeffkaplan.com/my-coaching-approach/

https://en.wikipedia.org/wiki/Margaret_Sanger

https://positivepsychologyprogram.com/solution-focused-therapy/

https://www.gurus.org/dougdeb/Courses/bestsellers/Celestine/Insights.htm

https://finance.yahoo.com/news/why-youre-thinking-networking-wrong-184500426.html

https://articles.spiritsciencecentral.com/balancing-male-female-energy/

https://www.linkedin.com/pulse/empowering-your-employees-isnt-top-priority-should-boyd-parker/?articleId=9048894242029785928